The Universal Power of YOU

Alan Di Felice

BALBOA
PRESS

A DIVISION OF HAY HOUSE

Balboa Press books may be ordered through booksellers or by contacting:

Balboa Press
A Division of Hay House
1663 Liberty Drive
Bloomington, IN 47403
www.balboapress.com
1-(877) 407-4847

Because of the dynamic nature of the Internet, any web addresses or links contained in this book may have changed since publication and may no longer be valid. The views expressed in this work are solely those of the author and do not necessarily reflect the views of the publisher, and the publisher hereby disclaims any responsibility for them.

The author of this book does not dispense medical advice or prescribe the use of any technique as a form of treatment for physical, emotional, or medical problems without the advice of a physician, either directly or indirectly. The intent of the author is only to offer information of a general nature to help you in your quest for emotional and spiritual well-being. In the event you use any of the information in this book for yourself, which is your constitutional right, the author and the publisher assume no responsibility for your actions.

Any people depicted in stock imagery provided by Thinkstock are models, and such images are being used for illustrative purposes only.
Certain stock imagery © Thinkstock.

ISBN: 978-1-4525-3985-0 (sc)
ISBN: 978-1-4525-3986-7 (e)

Printed in the United States of America

Balboa Press rev. date: 12/14/2011

Preface

My Name is Alan Di Felice, the author of the Universal Power of You.

Before I ever read a self help or spiritually based book I began to notice and realize that life wasn't a random act of circumstances, events and coincidences. Back in the late 90's I started to realize, mainly through the observation of others, that life brings you what you are asking for in terms of how you are thinking and subsequently feeling, talking, acting and behaving, in other words what you are consistently putting your attention on.

These observations were in relation to people who were mainly close to me in my life, family, friends and so on, and what they wanted from life, their current attitude towards their wants and their achieving of them. I'd observed that those who were quite easy going and didn't over think things seemed to be doing well, while others in an anti-relaxed, aggressive, impatient and over analytic state of mind weren't achieving their wants as easily, if at all - I was one of them.

As I observed how other people became a little more relaxed and reverted from not having their attention on not having what they wanted, I began to notice that life began to respond to them more favourably, and from that observation I concluded I should let go of the things I wanted and see what would happen.

When I began to practice letting go and to be just happy with where I was in life, the things I wanted that others had achieved and where necessary the means to afford them, now began to flow into my life. The new car, the holidays, new career opportunities, better financial success, new relationships, my first house and so on.

15 or so years on, and after reading many books, all good in their own way, I found my mind to be too cluttered and overloaded with information. I'd taken the simple equation that allowed life to work easily for me and made it complex. So I went back to what I knew worked, taking many things out of the equation, quietening my mind, allowing my body to relax, and coming to the understanding and realization of something I've inherently always known, I am the Universal Power of Me, I am the one creating all my life experiences, all the ups and all the downs, and so when I truly got that, the idea to write a book and share my knowledge came about.

Introduction

The Universal Power of You, is a book dedicated to helping you improve your life or aspects of your life in all areas.

It is my intention though the teachings in this book to share and in still the benefits of my learning's, my knowledge and my life experiences with you and to help you improve and better understand life, especially your life and the relationship you have with yourself in relation to everything you have going on in your life experience.

This book will give you not only the basis but also the details of how to improve your life in all areas. The teachings in this book can be universally applied, not only to your life, but to the lives of those you wish to share and practice the teachings of this book with.

In this book you will learn what is at the basis of everything that exists, you will learn and understand the physical and non-physical universe we live in and how the simultaneously coexist. You will achieve a higher state of awareness of how you interact with everything around you and how through your mind and the mindset that supports your life experience to date are creating your reality, both at a non-physical vibrational level and at the physical level of manifestation.

Your will acquire a true understanding of the limitless power of your thought, its limiting or limitless ability to create, and how to use your feelings to assess the appropriateness and correctness of how you are thinking in relation to what you are getting or how your life is playing out.

You will better understand the success of your relationships with people, health, prosperity, happiness, money and much more as this book begins to help you understand your relationship with yourself.

You will learn to release negative experiences in your life and begin to replace them with positive ones as you learn the Art of Forgiveness and the Power of Forgetting, and this will have a hugely positive impact on your upcoming life experiences.

You will learn how to look at the success in others that you want and replicate that into your life, by celebrating the success of others, and understanding that the emotional welling being of your relationships, is the oil that allows the law that brings all of what you want together for you.

Most of all you will learn to understand and more importantly, appreciated the incredible diverse, varying and contrasting environment in which you coexist with all other beings and things. As you will get that it is the diversity, the variance and the contrast which creates desire and desire is the fuel of life.

Contents

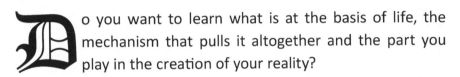

A note to you, the reader...

Do you want to learn what is at the basis of life, the mechanism that pulls it altogether and the part you play in the creation of your reality?

Then this is the book for you, for an investment of your time and the practicing of this knowledge, applied in an easy and fun loving way, you will begin to get and then understand who and the power of who you really are, and then transform all areas of your life, easily.

This book has been written so that it doesn't overload the reader with information but nonetheless will give you all the information you require to move your life in the directions that you want. The font type, size and line spacing was chosen carefully so that it is easy on the reader's eye and allows the reader to read and absorb the information easily.

Read this book slowly and absorb each word, there is no hurry here. As you read, breathe in and out slowly and gently, and allow your breathing to sync up with the easy rate of reading that you establish.

The guarantee of the degree of success or the degree of improvement that you desire in any area of your life lies completely within you, this book is a tool designed and written to help you improve areas of your life and to achieve your desires.

As you read and re-read this book and practice and re-practice its teachings, keep your mind free and open.

Thank You for buying the Universal Power of You.

To Your Happiness, Success & Wellbeing,

Enjoy!

Alan.

OK, lets you and I begin...

Energy

As we start this book, it is necessary for you to understand what is at the basis of all life, indeed what is at the basis of all that is physical and non-physical.

At the basis of everything is energy, energy and how if moves (vibrates), is what and specifically, an understanding here will make the reading, the content and the understanding of you, and life more comprehensible, and how to apply the knowledge contained in this book to all aspects of your very diverse and magnificent life.

If we start with what we know as the physical universe and begin to break it down, we see that within the physical universe we have galaxies, then solar systems, planets, minerals which are made up of particles, particles can be broken down to the atomic level, then the sub-atomic level and below that level is pure energy. It is at the sub-atomic level that solidity begins to cease to exist. At this level what exists is information and energy.

If we look at the human body and begin to break it down, we see that it is made up of organs, bones and fluid. Organs can be broken down in to cells, cells are broken down in to molecules, and molecules are broken down into atoms, atoms into protons, neutrons and electrons. Protons, neutrons and electrons are then broken down into Quanta (Quantum – singular). Below the quantum level we have the existence of wave packets which comprise of an infinite set of component waves. These waves contain the existence of all possibilities and probabilities. These waves are made up of vibrational energy and this vibrational energy is what effects the manifestation of matter.

So now we have the beginnings of an understanding, that everything comes down to one common denominator, and that is energy.

All matter is made up of energy, so you too are one big massive charge of energy.

Did you know that each cell in your body can hold up to the equivalent of 600 pages of text, and your body depending on its size can have up to 100 trillion cells? (To put 100 trillion into perspective, if you were to count to 100,000,000,000,000 taking 1 second per number, it would take you 3 million, 168 thousand and 800 hundred years.)

A lot of these cells contain the genes and other information needed to make up your physical being. This genetic information is found in the nucleus of the cell, the control center that keeps all the material together in one place. The nucleus stores its genetic material in packages called chromosomes.

Most people have 46 chromosomes in each cell—23 come from their mother and 23 from their father. These two sets of chromosomes match up to form 23 pairs.

Each chromosome is made up of genes. Genes contain the information used by other parts of the cell to make proteins, the body's building blocks. Proteins make up the structure of your organs and tissues, and they are also needed for your body's chemical functions. Each protein performs a specific job in different types of cells, and the information for making at least one protein is contained in a single gene.

Genes are made up of various lengths of DNA, which contains four chemicals, which are adenine, guanine, cytosine, and thymine. These chemicals align up to form strands of code.

The gene's chemical code for a protein contains the instructions for creating the protein. The instructions for making the protein are inside the cell's nucleus, but the parts that actually make the protein are outside the nucleus. To send the instructions to the protein-producing areas of the cell, the gene reads the chemical code and rewrites it into a new form. The new form is then sent out of the cell's nucleus to make proteins.

Just imagine how much information your body holds, all the instructions, the data and the know how to create, grow, maintain and heal you.

So not only are you one big mass of energy, you are also one massive walking, talking, intelligent and living information and memory bank.

EXPERIMENTAL FUN

A True Reflection of YOU – look at who you really are.

Stand back about 15 feet from a mirror. Now try and shift your focus of sight as if looking through your reflection.

Now let your eyes go slightly out of focus. Allow 10-15 seconds for this.

You should see the opposite of a shadow around you, something like the transparent vapour trails you see when an aeroplane is taking off.

This is the energy leakage from your body. This is the Energy life force that supports your physical being from the sub atomic level up. This is the essence and evidence of the non-physical part of you – say HELLO to all of yourself.

The Physical Universe

The physical part of life is made up of the stuff that we can see, hear, touch, taste and smell. Our five senses help and guide us as we interact with other objects, people and things that we call tangible.

When we touch an object, the electrons that surround the nucleus of an atom contained in that object push against one another, as does the nucleus of our atoms push against one another, and this gives us the sense of the physical feeling of that object. How hard or soft that object is, the texture it holds, and how it feels to our touch.

As we interact within this physical universe, there is always an exchange of energy between the objects interacting with one another, and this feedback is translated by our senses and interpreted by our brain.

All these atoms are moving, pulsating, vibrating at different frequencies. So everything is vibration, and this is what our senses do, they translate vibration, and through this translation we perceive what we call our physical universe.

As mentioned before, at the sub-atomic level exists information and energy, this is the melting of the physical into the non-physical. At the non-physical level, information, intelligent information, consciousness and mass consciousness of thought exists.

The physical part of life which is known as matter, and matter, through the manipulation of molecules, can be changed into different forms. The physical part of life is one of manipulation, manipulation of energy, and this is the ultimate illusion, that our physical senses perceive as our physical universe and physical reality.

The Non Physical Universe

The non-physical part of life, is the part of life that we mostly don't see or perceive through sight or touch. However, we all do have a strong awareness of that which we can't see or feel through sight or touch. Sounds and smells aren't tangible objects in relation to sight or touch; however we know they exist as our ears translate the vibration of sound and our nose translates the vibration of smell. Similarly, objects that we can touch and see are made up of a myriad of particles at various levels which are vibrating, and our eyes and touch translate this vibration into what we would call solid, tangible physical objects.

Everything that is physical comes from that which is non-physical, or to put it another way, all matter comes from anti-matter and that matter is built up from the sub-atomic level.

So in relation to you, what is the non-physical? Well, this is the spirit of who you are. This is the part of you that exists at the non-physical level; this is the ultimate reality of who you really are.

You are a non-physical being and part of that non-physical being is now focused physically. The non-physical part of you is eternal and it is the energy, the conscious energy of this non-physical being that supports your physical being. If the part of you that you see staring back at you in the mirror is the matter, then the non-physical part of you is the anti-matter.

A very simple way of understanding physical and non-physical, matter and anti-matter and the relationship between the two, is to get a piece of paper, fold it in half and cut out a square. Now you have a square physical piece of paper, but you also have a square non-physical hole too. The square cut out piece now exists from the non-physical square hole and vice versa.

The non-physical is what supports the physical, for out of the non-physical, the physical is born and simultaneously co-exists. The non-physical, is the ultimate reality of who you, and who we all are, and through this non-physical energy we co-exist as one. The physical part of who we are, whether we are talking about human beings, animals, plants, rocks, planets etc., is the ultimate illusion of who we are, for our true reality is non-physical, and it is at the non-physical reality level, that we initiate and create both our non-physical and physical life experiences. However, it is important to point out that through our physical existence and focusing on our desires, wants and goals, that we add to everything that exists both physically and non-physically and so the universe expands through this process.

Vibration

e live in a vibration-ally based, energy based universe, that is everything that exists is moving, pulsating and in motion at every level, from the cells in your body to the energy that has created our universe. All vibrations have a frequency, and as those frequencies match up, they begin to attract to one another, exactly the same way as setting your VHF or your UHF signal when tuning in your TV. In order to get a specific TV station the frequencies must match. This is how attraction works, it's very simple, when you think a thought it emits a certain frequency, and thoughts that match that frequency attract to one another, other thoughts of the same frequency or vibration.

Have you ever wondered why, when you think a certain way on a given subject, the next thing you know, you have this spiral of thoughts that are similar, flying around in your head, well now you have the answer. This is attraction at work and thoughts attract similar thoughts and that leads to thought form.

Think of all of our communication devices that we have, they are all based on and mimicking this, we just haven't taken the time to observe it, and make the connection to how we get the things in life we get.

Let us look at this a little more closely, let us go back to the beginning of the book when we talked briefly about energy. Energy is vibrational too; it is pulsating in everything that exists. You too are vibration, both the physical and non-physical part of you. Every part of your being has a vibration, including and very importantly, the thoughts that you think.

So, the thoughts that you think are vibrational, they have a frequency and frequencies that match up attract one another. This is important to remember as you read the next pages.

If 100 people were put into a room and left there for a period of time, and you were to check in on them from time to time, you would begin to observer that those 100 people were forming into groups. As time would move on, you would observe that those groups would split down into smaller groups.

After a period of time, if you came back to those 100 people and started to talk with them in their groups, you would observe that the people in each group had similar characteristics. In other words these people were like minded.

Being likeminded means that people, who think similarly to one another, are therefore also attracted and drawn to one another.

Remember vibrations that match, frequencies that match, attract to each other, and it is via this attraction process that everything is brought and assembled together, through the vibrational frequencies, that all things, all elements of this universe, both non-physical and physical are emitting.

Law of Attraction

Law of Attraction is the universal mechanism that brings everything together. It is via this law that our thought process is the process by which we all create our reality. When you think a certain thought, Law of Attraction matches that thought, by offering you another one that matches the frequency (vibration) of the thought you are thinking.

Basically, Law of Attraction means that like energy attracts like energy, and from a physical human consciousness perspective, the beginning of this attraction process is at the thought level.

As you begin to think a certain way on a subject, Law of Attraction offers you a similar thought, the more you think the thought or similar thoughts, the more you are offered back, your thinking on a subject becomes habitual, which then evolves into a belief system, and as this is happening, if you pay attention to what is going on around you, on a subject that you are giving your attention to, you will begin to notice, that at the physical level things are beginning to change in relation to how you are thinking about them.

Look out also for those things you call coincidences, this is part of the evidence that this life you lead, and this universe you live in, is giving you insight into what is coming into your life experience.

Let's use the car scenario, give your attention to a car that you want and how good it would be to have it. Then notice throughout the day how many times you see that car. Later that day you may be talking with someone and the subject of cars comes up, you talk about the car that you like, and it turns out that the person you are talking to knows someone with that car that you want. This is the evidence of the Law of Attraction at work. It's important to recognize that this Law works for everything, so initially it's worth your while observing the way things are in all areas of your life, and then asking the question, is this how I'd like all these things to be? And if not, then you need to look at how you are thinking in relation to each area, and then looking at how you would like each area to be, and from that point moving forward by adapting your thinking on each area.

At this stage it is important to be aware of the emotional feelings you have in relation to the thoughts that you think, as these emotional feelings that are offered back to you on any subject you are thinking about has magnificent value. Ask the question when you are thinking on any subject, "how does this way of thinking make me feel", is it positive or negative?

A little later we will look at the reason as to the importance of those emotional feelings.

Now let's make a comparison here with the Law of Attraction to the Law of Gravity. When people begin to try to understand the Law of Attraction they have a tendency to put a lot of their attention on it, the trick here is to just accept that this is how it is.

You don't think about the Law of Gravity every time you go out for a walk because you know that it is there doing its job without you having to give any thought to it.

If you were going out to your friend's house you wouldn't stare at the ground as you walked to check that Gravity was still working, if you did that you wouldn't be paying attention to where or the direction in which you were going, and you'd probably never get to their house because you wouldn't be focused on the outcome of your journey, and this is another tip, you need to positively focus on what it is that you want, and go in that direction by paying attention to how you feel, and observing what is going on around you in relation to what you want, and not focusing on the law that will bring it to you.

One important thing to know here and this is probably the most important aspect for you to know, is that Law of Attraction doesn't discern between what you want and don't want. Law of Attraction gives you what you are putting your attention and thought on, Law of Attraction doesn't know if you want it or not, only you know that, and this is the purpose and importance of paying attention to how you feel. How you feel is the guidance within you. *Tip* – do your best to feel good as often as you can, this will enhance the Law of Attraction process in relation to what you do want, and you will enjoy **yourself** all the more on the way to the things you desire. This will help raise your vibration (vibe) too. The things you want come a lot easier when you have a high vibration (giving off a good vibe, being in a good mood).

Yourself is all of who you are, not just the body part. When you are enjoying yourself, all of who you are is aligned with the vibration of joy, happiness and love and you will feel great.

Thoughts

A lot of people don't give a whole lot of consideration to the thoughts that they are thinking. They just see them as images, ideas, or non-consequential things floating around in their head without any pending results or consequences. People believe that it's their actions that create what they have in their life experience and while they would be correct in thinking that from their perspective and understanding, they never consider that no action happens without prior thought.

I think of something that I want to do and then based on my circumstances, my situation or my beliefs around my thinking I carry out a subsequent action. Well that is the case, but there is a very bigger picture that most people aren't aware of or haven't figured out.

Your thoughts are very powerful non-physical creative forces that do create the life experience you are living. Stop and think (give thought) to this for a moment. Your thinking is affected by something you are remembering, imagining or observing.

When you are thinking positively in relation to a certain subject or area in your life (this could be your job, relationships, a car, a house, money, circumstances or events) you begin to see the benefit of this as the outcome of this positive way of thinking, is that the way you want something to be, actually begins to happen in the way you want it.

When you are thinking positively and appreciating the good in the person you share your life with, you will begin to see how the relationship feels a lot easier, it begins to improve, life on the subject of your partner just begins to feel better and go better for no apparent reason.

When you are thinking negatively about the person you share your life with you begin to see that things don't go as nicely as you would want them to. They may seem unresponsive to you, they seem distant, unappreciative and argumentative with you and this doesn't feel good to you.

When you are thinking positively on any subject you feel good, when you are thinking negatively on any subject, you don't feel so good. We'll talk a little later on the feeling aspect of this but for now just pay attention to how you feel, on any subject or area of your life that you are giving thought to.

Your thinking is a powerful limiting or limitless force, which allows you to create the life you want or to hold you back from creating the life you want. It is all really about you and your thought.

Henry Ford said "If you think you can, or you think you can't, you're right", in other words if you say "yes" to yourself, that "I can do" that, be that or have that, that initiates a belief in you that takes you in the direction of what you want and it feels good. If you say "no", "I can't do" that or "I couldn't do" that, then you stop dead in your tracks and in that moment you've started to set a limiting belief, that you can't have or do or be something and it immediately feels bad.

The only person who can think for you is you. If you are observing something or listening to someone, and what is happening or being said generates a thought or a pattern of thinking and it feels bad to you, what you need to do, is either change how you are looking and subsequently thinking about what you are observing or listening to, so that it feels better, or alternatively take your attention away from what you are observing or listening to so it doesn't enter into or affect or influence your way of thinking.

On the other side of this, is to look for positive things to observe that are in line with your way of thinking. For example, you see someone driving a car that you like and you think to yourself, oh how I'd love one of those and fair play to that chap or girl who is driving it. Wouldn't it be great to have a go in one of those? Well maybe I can, I can go to a dealer and arrange a test drive and really see what it is like to drive and how it **feels** to be in one. And then maybe you might imagine what it would be like to actually own one and how you could drive it whenever you want, take your friends or the girl/boyfriend out for a spin, showing it off and why not. Feel how good it feels to think you can have this, imagine how it feels.

Albert Einstein said "Imagination is the preview of all things to come".

When you are giving thought (thinking, imagining, pondering, dreaming) of the things that you want, and you don't know how it's going to come about, where the money is going to come from, who will be involved in helping to bring it about – don't give any thought to this aspect of the thing you want as you will begin to think negatively about it, and your belief on what you want will begin to change, become limited and then negative. Again the trick here is always pay attention to how you are feeling about what you are giving your thought to, this is very, very, important.

Have you ever heard the expression "I think, therefore I am", well let me add my own flavour to this, what that means is, as you give thought to something, you are in the becoming of, or in the becoming of having that very thing you are giving your thought to, so pay attention to how the thought feels, as the feeling lets you know the appropriateness and correctness of your thoughts in relation to what you want.

EXPERIMENTAL FUN

(The Thought Processor – take some time for positive thinking)

Pick a quiet time and a spot where you can go each day or night. Get yourself into a nice thinking, feeling state – maybe listen to some music that makes you feel good.

Now sit down and take few minutes to allow your mind and body to quiet down and relax.

Take a deep breath and allow your lungs to completely fill up with air. Hold the breath for a count of three and then slowly breathe out to the count of three, letting your lungs completely deflate. Repeat this process three times allowing your mind to clear and your body to relax.

Now take a subject (money, house, relationship, health) you are interested in having or improving and slowly, gently begin to think about and imagine having it, consider how good it feels to have it, what would you do with this new or improve thing or situation, how would your life be different.

Do this each day on subject after subject and repeat it on each subject when you feel like it, spend ten to fifteen minutes on this each time on each subject, or for as long as it feels good or it is pleasing to you. Pay attention to how you are feeling. If you start to begin to feel a little negative, stop and consider the direction your thought process (thinking) is going in. If you can't revert back easily to a more positive state of thinking, exit the Thought Processor and come back another day.

Tip – The best time to do this exercise is at night before you go to sleep, this is because the conscious mind is preparing to calm down and at the same time you impress what you want on to the sub-conscious mind. As you sleep the conscious mind isn't offering any contradictory thoughts in relation to what you want.

The Creations of Thought

Everything starts with a thought, everything that you see around you that has been created by us (humans) all started with an initial thought or idea.

All thoughts currently exist and it's the collating of thoughts which creates thought form and it is this forming of thought that produces new combinations of thought and this is what is called the creative thought process.

It is through this process that creation is born, new things are invented, new things in relation to you are manifested and your life, this world and this universe expands.

If you take something simple to start with, the chair you are sitting on for instance, someone had to have the thought of what that chair would look like. The chair would have been designed from the imagination of the person. The materials that were used to make the chair would have had to have started with thought and from there designed and manufactured. The equipment to manufacture the materials would have had to have started with a thought; the sum of the components that make up the equipment would have had to have started with a thought.

The way the chair would be manufactured and assembled, would have had to have started with a thought.

The transport used - trucks, ships, aeroplanes and all those components and the brining together of all those components, all started with thought. The shop and all the material used to build the shop, decorated it, light it, heat it and maintain it, all started with thought.

Take a step back for a moment and look at the biggest ships, sky scrapers, damns, bridges, power plants, space ships and stations, and think of everything that has to be thought about from the design and engineering of the final product and all its components, to the assembly, testing of all the systems that support these magnificent things that we take for granted, and now you get a sense of the power of the thought that each of us possesses.

Imagine a huge cruise ship, thought had to go into the design of each type of nut and bolt that is used to bolt the ship together, thought had to go into the stress that each of those nuts and bolts that were used, depending on what each type of nut and bolt was going to be used for, and what type of conditions those nuts and bolts would be exposed to, and the varying environments that those different types of conditions would occur in, and that is just the nuts and bolts. Now think about everything that goes into a ship, all the components and the components that make up those components; engines, oil, fuel, cooling and heating systems, computer systems that regulate everything and the software too. The cabins, the beds, the bed linen, showers, toilets, air conditioning, kitchens, utensils, communications systems, radar, and so on and so on, it's absolutely endless – now just think of all that thought and all the fantastic things it creates. All the power of that thought comes through YOU. The most powerful source of everything on this planet, in this universe, comes through you and we take it for granted, without usually giving a moment's thought to it, how ironic is that?

Habitual Thoughts
& Thinking

Habitual thoughts or thinking is just you having formed a certain way of thinking around different subjects and areas within your life.

Many of us have been thought to think a certain way on different subjects and have been strongly influence by our parents, teachers, friends, colleagues, the church, our government, the media and those around us, who interact with us on a regular basis.

With all of this interaction and influence, especially as children and young adults, how we think has been programmed to a large extent by others.

Our habitual thinking then forms our beliefs, which in turn develops into a belief system around different subjects.

If you're thinking and beliefs are serving you well, then that's fine and good, for you are getting what you want in life and you should be intentionally creating your life experience through how you are thinking.

If however you don't have what you want in life, then this is down to a limited way of thinking and a limited belief system.

The good news is you can change how you think in relation to anything at anytime, however this does take a little effort, persistence and time on your behalf for you to establish a new thought pattern in relation to whatever subject you are giving your attention to.

Again you can gauge how you are thinking and how your belief systems are working for or against you, by paying attention to how you are feeling on all subjects and the things that you want out of life.

If your thinking and beliefs don't feel so good, then the first thing not to do is beat up on yourself, your current state of thinking and believing is where it is and that is just fine, because by recognising that your thinking and believing is not bringing you what you want, by paying attention to how you feel, and observing what is coming and being retained in your life, you have now taken the initial and the biggest step in moving in the direction to being able to change your thinking pattern and the associated beliefs you have.

When each of us are born we don't have a conscious way of thinking, we all start equally with a blank slate. So, on any subject you can wipe the slate clean and begin writing what you want on it, what you want to think and believe on any subject.

If you look around the environment you live in, in your job, housing estate, county or country and you see an environment where all you see are things not going so well, or going badly, this is because you've been taught to see things predominately that way. If this is the way you predominately see things, then even if you move to a much better environment, you will begin to seek out the bad things, even if there aren't any bad things, you will create them in your mind, find things that are good to actually play down, then moan about, and then say, oh look how bad things are here too.

However, if you've been taught to look around you and see all the good that there is, no matter where you are or who you are interacting with, you will seek out the good and even if you are living in a slum, you will notice that the sun is shining, the birds are singing, people are getting on with their lives, interacting and laughing with one another, it all depends on how you want to look at it.

If what you are looking at doesn't feel good to you then change how you are looking at it (thinking about it) and what you are looking at will change. Don't put your attention (your thought) on things you don't want, as a famous person once said, "Turn the other cheek" – Do you get this?

Think about this statement and what it actually means, go on give it a little thought, you will find the answer – Tip, ask the question what does this mean and then try and quiet your mind and see if the answer comes.

Albert Einstein once said, "The world we have created is a product of our thinking; it cannot be changed without changing our thinking." This statement also applies to the world (the reality) that you have created for yourself.

My Powerful Mind

The mind is a very powerful source of influence over you. You have been programming and teaching it all of your life.

It contains all your associated thoughts about everything that you have experienced.

Your mind is a by-product of how you have been thought to think, or how you have learned to think, about everything that you have going on in your life and in your environment.

It has learnt to associate events, circumstances and experiences with particular ways of thinking which causes you to respond, act and behave in certain ways, this could be positive or negative behaviours depending on how you have programmed, or allowed yourself to be programmed in different areas of your life.

All of your likes, dislikes, anxieties, excitements, fears and enthusiasms are all in your mind. It is through your mind that you perceive and see things in a certain way. It is your thought based mind that creates your reality.

Cherish the mind that servers you well, these will be the thoughts that have a positive influence in how you look at things in life.

Where there is negativity, it is your job to start changing your mind in relation to these things, or areas that your mind holds you back in, or upsets your state of being.

Empty your mind of all things that do not serve you positively. When you do this your mind becomes free and you will feel the benefit of that, as you will feel more at ease mentally and physically.

Read The Mind Cleanser on the next pages and start practicing this tool, but first read the chapter "My Emotional Feelings".

THE MIND CLEANSER

Before you begin this exercise you need to understand that it will take some practice for this exercise to become natural to you, in other words, when it becomes natural to you, you will be able to do it without having to think too much about the steps below. So be prepared to give this a few attempts until you begin to experience the benefit of it. Remember there's no rush.

Firstly find a quiet and comfortable place to sit or lie down, a place where you won't be disturbed and at a time of the day where you have thirty minutes to yourself.

Step one – (5 Minutes)

Firstly practice taking slow deep breaths, allow your lungs to fill up completely and your chest to rise fully. Hold each breath for the count of three, and then allow your lungs to slowly and completely deflate to the count of three.

Once you become comfortable and used to doing step one, so that you can do it without thinking about it, then follow on to step two.

Step two – (5 Minutes)

Take in a slow deep breath and on the exhale say to yourself, "My mind is calm, clear and relaxed". As you do this, allow your mind to gently and slowly clear.

Repeat step two until you feel your mind feeling lighter, which it will, as you release any negative thoughts.

Note: You may experience a tingling or fizzing sensation around the fore or crown of your head.

Step three – (15 – 20 Minutes)

Now switch from saying "My mind is calm, clear and relaxed" to saying my body is "relaxed and at ease" while continuing to breathe.

As you do step three begin to imagine a warm wave of relaxation running down your body, from your head, down your face (forehead, eyebrows, eyelids, nose, checks, mouth, lips & chin), your neck, your shoulders, down your arms into your hands and fingers, down your back, your torso, your hips, your buttocks, into your legs, knees, ankles, heals, feet and toes.

As you imagine this warm wave of relaxation running down your body, let each part of your body go limp and imagine all the tension, stress and negative energy being released into the universe from your physical body.

Do this exercise for fifteen to twenty minutes (more if you wish).

As you practice this you will feel the weight of your physical body on the chair or bed as it achieves total relaxation.

\When you complete this exercise, your mind and body will feel light and refreshed and you will most likely experience a strong tingling sensation all over and around your physical body.

When you begin to become familiar with performing this exercise, you may experience the sensation of your consciousness becoming separate from your physical body, don't be alarmed. Enjoy it! There may be other things you experience too, however I'll let you discover these experiences for yourself – it's all good.

My Emotional Feelings

Even when they're bad, they're Great!

IECGS (Integrated Emotional Communication & Guidance System)

Your IECGS, what exactly is this. Well, have you ever wondered why on earth we have feelings and emotions? The answer is very simple; this is in essence a communication device. Your IECGS lets you know, by how your emotions are feeling, the appropriateness and correctness of the thoughts you are giving thought to in relation to what you want, or the subject you are thinking about.

This requires a little explaining and some realisation and recognition on your part, that there is a whole lot more to you than the physical body you see when you look in the mirror. You may want to refer back to Experimental Fun **A True Reflection of YOU** earlier in the book in chapter one, Energy, to get a grasp of this.

Each of us has depending on how we label it, a soul, an inner being, an astral body, a light body, a sub-conscious, a side to us that has existed longer than you could consciously remember, or indeed, may be able to comprehend at this point.

This non-physical side of us is the sum of all of our life experiences, both physical and non-physical and is connected to all that is, so our non-physical selves have access to a very broad and exact perspective and understanding of all of life, and how it works. How cool is that – when you get what this means and how it feels by reading this book you'll know. But to touch on what this means at this point, this means very simply that by paying attention to how you feel, you will know moment to moment, minute to minute, day to day, if the thoughts you are thinking and their vibrational frequency they are emitting, are bringing to you via the Law of Attraction, in the direction of the things you want to have, or do, or be in your life, or are your thoughts bringing you in the opposite direction. Now you know why this book is called The Universal Power of You. For whether you believe it or not, you are creating your life experience and the reality in which you live, and as you do, you add on to all that is, and this universe through your observation of life, dreaming of life, putting your attention and thought on any given subject, expands this universe.

Every thought you think adds to all other thoughts that have been thought by you, thoughts then become thought form which leads to words and then to actions and through this simple process, life and the universal platform in which we exist and operate expands. Both positive and negative thoughts add to everything, one doesn't cancel the other, for thought is energy adding to itself constantly and consistently.

So emotion, simply put, is Energy in Motion (very fast, fluid and non-resistant Energy in Motion), and how this emotion feels is the way the non-physical side of you, communicates with you in your physical being. Negative emotional energy is non-resistance, it may not feel good but the resistance is not in the emotion, it is in the thought that sets up the emotional feedback to you (physically) from you (non-physically).

The reason this is, is that there is far too much chatter, too much noise going on inside your conscious mind for the non-physical side of you, to communicate with the physical side of you through your mind, so this is achieved through emotional feelings. It is said that, "feelings are the language of the soul".

In order to benefit from the communication of your emotions, the more in touch you need to be with your feelings. The way you achieve this, is to consciously ask yourself, how do I feel in relation to something you are giving your attention to?

The more positive you are in your thinking and paying attention to the emotional response, the clearer the communication will be.

Let's look at the opposite of this for a minute, to help you understand how effectively you are allowing your connection to your emotions.

If someone is constantly doing something bad, but doesn't feel any negative emotion in relation to their thoughts or actions, that is because they have in a sense unconsciously unplugged themselves from the feedback they receive from their inner self, and remember, the inner you, is the part of you that is infinite intelligent source energy, constantly flowing to you, around you and through you.

To put this another way, when someone is feeling negative but doesn't recognize the feeling as being negative, what this means is the person has become so used to feeling this way, that it actually feels normal, so the emotional feeling goes unheard. This is similar to tuning out when someone is speaking to you, you know they are talking to you but you're not hearing what they are actually saying to you.

However, when someone who has unplugged themselves, puts the plug back into the socket and the connection is made again, they will begin to quite quickly experience the negative emotion in relation to the thoughts or actions, past, present or future that they have associated themselves with.

So the key to optimizing this guidance is to Believe in yourself, believe in your Inner You, trust in your Inner You and the feedback and communication you get, through the emotional feeling your Inner You offers you (the physical you).

To help you get this a little more and the importance of your emotional feelings and paying attention to those emotional feelings, let's make a comparison to physical feelings.

If you were standing by your fire in your house and you were beginning to get too warm, you would move away from (in the opposite direction of) the fire because you are beginning to feel physically uncomfortable, you wouldn't move in the direction of the fire, because you know by paying attention to how you physically feel in relation to the heat of the fire, that, that would be going in the wrong direction. The exact same principle applies to you paying attention to how your emotions feel to you. If your thinking on a certain subject is getting a little warm (negative thinking) and you want to feel relief from the heat, you need to change your direction of thought so that your emotional feeling begins to feel more comfortable to you.

The Ladder of Emotions

T here are two basic categories of emotion, one is positive and the opposite is of course negative. All emotions that exist fall into either of these two categories.

There are a wide variety of emotions, and these emotions that we feel, are always in a direct response to what or how we are thinking about something.

The degree of positive or negative thought that is been given to a subject will produce the equivalent emotion within us.

Again, this is how your soul, your inner you, your spirit, the non-physical part of who you are communicates with the physical being that you are also.

Next is a visual representation of the different types of emotions and where they sit on the emotional ladder.

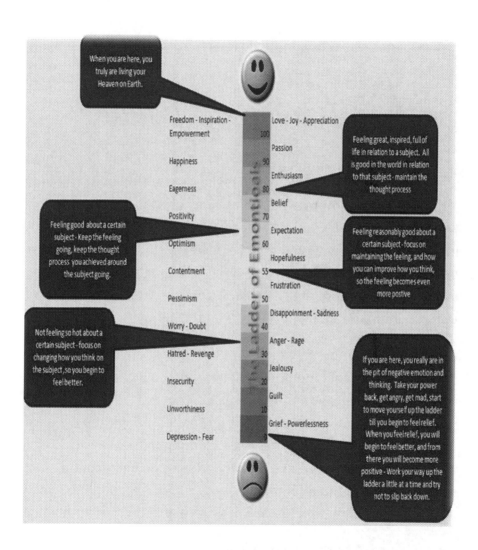

The Emotional Ladder

Pay attention to how IT feels. As you think a statement in relation to what you want out of life, pay attention to how it feels. When you recognise that you have an Inner You working with you and the power of this universe on your behalf, to deliver on what you ask for. Knowing and trusting that the Inner You, knows exactly how to get the things you want and then to offer guidance in bringing you to them.

As you become more in touch with the feeling of your emotions, you will begin to feel the power of who you really are, you will feel this in your lower abdomen mostly, however, over time you will feel the Inner You, make itself known to you though the physical sensations in your body. These sensations will feel like fizzing or tingling sensations and are initially present in and around your spinal area, but these sensations will extend throughout your physical being over time as you pay more attention to yourself.

Say to yourself, "I trust and believe in the power of who I really am, in all that I am".

NOW

This is where all my power is

ow is where all your power is. What does this mean? Everything that you will live in your future is being created now by how you are focusing your thoughts in relation to any area of your life.

The thoughts that you are giving most of your attention too, will result in the mix of the life experiences that you will have at sometime in your future.

You need to remember that you are thinking moment to moment right here and right now, so you also need to pay attention to how you are feeling right here and right now also. This is the key to controlling your thought process, and ensuring that you stay on track in relation to what you want to experience and live at some stage in your future.

Remember that life, the universe is responding to you in varying degrees, via the Law of Attraction based on the vibrational pull of the thoughts you are thinking, right here and right now.

Currency of Life

Everything that exists physically and non-physically has a vibrational frequency, when you begin to think of something, your thought begins to match that vibrational frequency, and by Law of Attraction you begin to attract that which you are thinking of into your life.

Thought is the true currency of life, so spend it abundantly and wisely. Only give thought to that which you want or pleases you.

Good Quality of Thought is the most valuable currency you can possess, as it is Thought that initiates the creation of all of your life experiences, the wanted ones and the not so wanted ones too.

Think of this another way, when you go into a shop, do you intentionally spend money on something that you know you don't like. Well I hope you wouldn't, I'd imagine you'd spend your money on something that you do want and the same goes for the thoughts you think.

Be choosy about the thoughts that you think

Success of Life

The true measurement of success is not the money, the cars, the houses, the magnificent life style or the relationships, the true measurement of success, the only and absolute measurement of success, is the joy and happiness you feel moment to moment.

The money, cars, houses, relationships, health and wellbeing are but a by-product of that joy and happiness that you feel. For in that positive place of feeling, there is no resistance to what you want, and all that you have desired through Thought (the currency you've spent) now must flow easily and abundantly into your life experience.

Who is the most successful person on this planet? Remember, there are plenty of ways to measure different types of success in relation to any subject, however, the person who possesses true success, is the person who has realized happiness in all aspects of their life, by deciding that no matter what is happening, or has happened, who is doing or saying what, all that matters to them is how they feel, and all they want to feel regardless, is positively good and happy. <u>You get to choose how you want to feel</u>.

There is no such thing as failure, only degrees of Success

If there is something in life you want to achieve and you set a target and a timeline but don't achieve what you wanted in relation to the target or timeline you've set, does this mean you have failed?

The answer is no, because depending on how you look at it, ultimately there is no such thing as failure, what there is, is degrees of success in relation to what you want to achieve.

Ultimately there is no such thing as Failure, only degrees of Success. If you have not yet achieved what you wanted or desired, the best thing to do to keep you on track is to look at the success you've had so far. Looking at it this way puts you in a more positive frame of mind, look at how well you've done and applaud yourself for your success so far.

While failure (not yet achieving your desire) is part of success, success is never part of failure.

Everything you have experienced in life, wanted and unwanted, completely or partially achieved is the evidence of your total success to date in relation to those experiences. What that means is, you can only succeed and the reason you can only succeed is because life is responding to how you are thinking. If you've had an unfavourable result or outcome, it's how you've been thinking on a subject that has successfully brought you to the outcome you are now experiencing (wanted or unwanted). It may not be the outcome you wanted or intended, but how you've been thinking in relation to what you wanted or not wanted has brought you there.

Allowance

Letting it all just happen. . .

Allowing what you desire is you spending your currency wisely. This is the ability not to think negatively in relation to what you desire.

For instance, if you want a new car, then you must think and feel what it would be like to have that new car, as opposed to thinking about the fact that you want it but don't have it.

Your focus can't be on the lack of what you desire as that will only bring you more lack. So you desire a new car, think about having it and see how that feels to you (if the feeling you get is a positive one, then you are spending your currency wisely, if it is a negative one, then you are not spending wisely, as how you feel, is always your guidance in understanding, if you are moving in the direction of your desire or in the opposing direction).

There are different ways in which to allow what you want.

By giving positive thought to the thing that you want without offering any negative thought (negative thought is you resisting the very thing that you want)

If you are getting really involved in the specifics of the thing that you want, and you are beginning to feel negative, then you need to step back a little, and think more generally of the thing that you want, and leave the specifics out.

When you get specific you are bringing in the who, the how, the what and the when into the equation, and at this point if you don't know the answer to this part of the equation, then this is why you will begin to feel some negative emotion.

If you think of the thing that you want and begin to feel negatively about it, forget about it, at least for a while, don't give any more thought to the thing that you want, and by doing that you will remove the resistance to it.

To want something and have it, you don't need to constantly think about it, when you first want it, the desire within you will be enough, and will begin to attract it into your life, how fast it comes or not, depends on the resistance that you setup or not in relation to that thing. All you need to really do here is just remain in a good feeling place.

When you are feeling good on whatever subject or for whatever reason, you are in alignment with yourself, and when you are in alignment you are allowing what you desire to show up in your physical life. Even if you are feeling good for no apparent reason your general alignment will allow the specifics of your desires to show up.

Having What You Want

You already have what you want, all your desires are created at the level of vibration first, they have to be, otherwise there would be nothing to start the attraction process at the non-physical level. So you see everything that you want, you already have, at the non-physical level.

Imagine all the things you've ever wanted you actually have, however, if you are not experiencing what you have already at the non-physical level at the physical level, then that is because you are holding yourself apart from experiencing it.

And the reason you are experiencing something or not at the physical level, depends on how you are thinking about it. Are you thinking positively or negatively, are the emotions that I'm experiencing, as I think about the things that I want, good feeling emotions or not?

To experience what you have at the non-physical level at the physical level, you must align the physical part of who you are, with the non-physical part of who you are. You do that by positively thinking about what you want, you do that by thinking in such a way that makes you feel good, that makes you feel happy, that puts you in a good mood and raises your level of vibration (vibe) which raises your Spirit. Now you are aligned and one with yourself and you will feel great, and all that you want is now yours to experience through your physical being.

Some spiritual wisdom - You came into this physical part of life, to experience at the physical level, all that you already know at the non-physical level. To put that into an example, you've known for a long time that we can fly, but in order to experience flying you must get onto a plane, the same way as to experience physical life you must come into a physical body.

Raising Your Vibration - Make a list of all things that makes you feel happy, that makes you laugh, and that makes you feel light and free. When you've done that, visit the list often, at least once a day to begin with and take the time to go through it, so it helps you feel good. When you feel good you feel light, there is a spring in your step, everything seems to be going well, and the sun is shining from the inside out. That's because you've raised your level of vibration (vibe).

All that has ever existed, exists primarily at the level of vibration, every vibration has its own frequency and vibrational frequency is the method by which attraction takes place. Everything that exists (events, circumstances, relationships, physical objects, etc.) has an opposite. This is a vibration-ally and attraction based universe, and at the base of this universe and all creation, is the co-creation and co-existence of all possibilities, and all of these possibilities (past, present and future) exist right now. Because you are vibrational too, just like everything else, all possibilities exist within you right now, so everything that you could every want, or desire, you have right now at the level of vibration.

The key here is to be aware of the opposites of the possibilities, and to only give your attention to the thing that you desire to manifest into your physical life experience. Remember you already have what you desire, to access it and manifest it, you must intend to only put your attention on the side of the thing you intend to manifest – a lot of people (unintentionally) put their attention on the opposite, or lack of what they desire, and because that already exists within you too, this is what they bring to the surface and is reflected into their physical life experience.

You could compare this to a console game, whereby all possibilities for that game exist within the program on that CD, and as you play the game you make choices, and those choices lead you in a certain direction in the game, either to a desired outcome or not.

DESIRE THAT, WANT THAT WHICH YOU KNOW YOU ALREADY HAVE

Entering into the Spirit of IT - Remember you have all that you desire, you have it at the level of vibration, and to bring it into the physical you must enter into the Spirit of it. And how do you do that, imagine it, pretend it, play with it, have fun in doing so, be easy, be happy and feel good about it, Love IT. Be that what you want to be, create the reality of it in your mind, imagine it and act it out – *Remember* – *"Imagination is the preview of all things to come"*.

You need to make the connection now that energy and spirit are the same, and now is a good time to say this to you. People have a tendency to resist what they want, because they for whatever reason, have a negative believe going on that being materialistic is not a good thing, or not a spiritual thing, but it very much is. If you are getting what is been told to you here, you will begin to realize that, that which is material exists at the level of spirit first, and the physical manifestation is a by-product or indeed the end product of that which is firstly spirit.

Your Keys to the Kingdom of Heaven

Your Thoughts are the non-physical part of who you are.

Your thoughts are part of the non-physical being that you are, your thoughts are the keys to your kingdom of heaven and thought was where heaven and earth were created.

Everything is created at the level of thought, and thought is energy in its purest and most powerful form, for it is thought that has created everything.

Energy flows through all matter, it supports all matter, and energy exists through an infinite array of vibrational frequencies that attract one another, and when combined determines the physical forms of matter.

Look at children as they play, having fun, imagining that they are someone different to who they currently are. See how they enter into the spirit of what they are playing at or doing. See how easily they do enter into the spirit of it, and how there is little or no resistance in them.

A parent may tell a child no to something they want, but their focus on the thing they want is brought to them anyway, may be through an uncle, a grandparent or an unexpected present.

Through their positive focus on what they want, they sync up with the vibrational frequency of what they want, and through the attraction process it is brought to them.

You see heaven and earth co-exist, just at a different rate of vibration, for all that is in heaven exists on earth too, as they are both one and the same, just opposites simultaneously co-existing. And all that you want is waiting for you in heaven and you call it forth through your asking for it, believing, having faith that it is yours, and when you do that, what you want appears in your physical experience, and you now have your little piece of heaven on earth.

Deliberate Creating or Auto Piloting

Deliberate creating is you deciding what you want in your life experience. It is you taking control of the thoughts that you are thinking, that are creating what you have in your life experience.

Auto piloting - For a lot of people, this is something they do automatically, that is they let their thoughts control how they think, by not understanding that they are on autopilot, and thinking randomly based on what they are observing around them, or remembering or thinking about something that may or may not happen in the future. As they are doing this, they are in the process of creating future life experiences. However, what they will create will depend on how much time they give to the thoughts they are thinking about, and to the intensity of those thoughts. Remember, you can tell the intensity of those thoughts you are thinking, by paying attention to how you are feeling, basically how does your gut feel. Tip – do a tummy test, remember, this is the non-physical side of you giving you feedback on how appropriate your thoughts are, that you are thinking in relation to what you want.

Controlling Your Thought Environment

When you think a thought ask yourself the question, is this something I want in my life experience, as the more attention that you give to a particular thought, which will become a thought pattern, and then a habitual thought, will eventually manifest into your life experience, and become part of your belief system, as the manifestation is now the proof of that. However, a lot of people don't put this puzzle together unless it is explained, like it is being explained now.

The thoughts that you constantly think today, are ones that have been programmed into your conscious way of thinking, from all manner of sources that you have <u>allowed</u> to influence how you think, and view things in the world today.

The other question is, does you current way of thinking in relation to a specific thing or area serve you, or not, is your way of thinking bringing you what you want in life in relation to that specific thing or area.

Controlling thought is not an easy thing to do, it takes practice, it takes awareness of what's rattling around inside your head. The best way to control your thoughts, is to control how you think, and how do you do that.

Take some time to document what you are giving your most thought to, this will vary, but I do guarantee you, that 80 percent of the thoughts that you think, are around the same things, day in and day out.

Catalogue these areas that you mainly think about. Now write down how you think about these areas. Now write down the corresponding feelings that you have to how you think about these areas. Do the feelings feel good, bad or mixed to you? Most likely you will have mixed feelings. Now identify the negative feelings on your list, and start to change how you think about a certain area until your feelings begin to improve. This may take a little time if you've had strong negative feelings towards something, however, as you improve how you think, and then how you feel, that area in your life will begin to improve, and you will see the evidence of that almost immediately, and the more you continue to improve how you think and subsequently feel, the more that area, situation, circumstance will improve too.

It's important to point out that your emotions don't create your life experience. People may worry that if they have strong negative emotion about something that they are creating something that they don't want quite quickly.

However this is not the case, the emotion is only the indicator not the creator, your emotions are the initiators of the creation of the things, events and circumstances, that will physically manifest into your life experience if you keep your thoughts on a given subject long enough.

The quickest way to attract something you want into your life is to get into the feeling place of it.

To get into the feeling place of something, you need to practice how it would feel by thinking about it. When you've practiced the positive thought of having something, and how it would feel, you can easily slip into the feeling place of it, without giving too much thought to it, and therefore remove the possibilities of setting up resistant thought – "Don't think, just feel it".

So there are differences here in relation to getting into a feeling place and to that of receiving emotional feedback, the feeling place of something you want is a positively charged place to be, emotional feedback, positive or negative is a quick and direct response to thoughts that you are thinking, I hope you are getting the difference. If not don't worry, you will, just give it a little time and don't think about it too much.

Let's try something here to help you get this, "Getting into the Feeling of IT". Think of something that you would really like to have, let's pretend it's a nice house, standing on its own grounds with beautiful manicured gardens, and so on, you get the idea.

Now your job is to imagine this lovely house you want, imagine walking around the gardens, down by the pool, up the patio made from beautiful Italian limestone, in through the double pine doors, walking through your magnificent kitchen, into the hallway that is laid with American Oak wooden floors, and so on.

You are imaging this to **be** in this very moment as if it has already happened. How would you feel as you walked around your incredible house, how would the carpet feel under your feet, how would the marble kitchen work tops feel to your touch, how would it feel to kick back and relax on your Nappa leather reclining armchair.

Now, to achieve what has been described above, you can't be putting the how, when, where's the money going to come from into it. You are going to perform the above exercise on whatever topic it is in relation to what you want in the way a 5, 6 or 7 year old would do it, from the pure positive place of imagining it. Leave all the stuff you don't know about out of it (how, when, who), and just put your attention on being in the moment of imagining it, as if this is how it is now at the physical level.

Once you achieve being able to purely imagine what you want, put an imaginary bubble around it, and the next time you think about what you want, just slip into that bubble where nothing else exists, only the thing you want.

When you perform this type of exercise, don't start looking for the evidence of where, or how, or is it coming, should I be taking some action, just trust that it is on its way, have a little faith and leave it at that.

However, be mindful of those things you call "coincidences" this will be life demonstrating to you that things are beginning to fall into place.

If the time comes for you to take some action in relation to what you want, you will feel the need to do something, pay attention to those little nudges you get in your abdomen area. That's the signal from the non-physical you to the physical you to do something, and you will know what that something is when the time comes. To put it another way, you will <u>feel</u> inspired into action.

Relax, Release & Allow

Getting yourself into a relaxed state is the key to achieving harmony with yourself, and the desires that you have.

When you are in a relaxed state of being, you, that is, your mind, body and soul are in alignment and you'll feel good throughout. Also, when you are in this state of being you are as closely aligned as you can be vibration-ally. You will never be completely vibration-ally aligned because your physical being, your mind and your soul (non-physical being) vibrate at different frequencies, however all three of you (who are actually one, as there is no real separation) can become very closely aligned.

When you are aligned vibration-ally, that is your mind, body, and soul, you release negative thought and therefore negative feelings, and when you do that, then you are in a true state of allowing and you feel very good, all seems well with the world and you feel a lot lighter in yourself. People may say there is a spring in your step or she looks like she's walking on air.

So how do you achieve this state of being, well with a little practice and patience it is quite easy. Remember the whole point of this exercise is to put you (yourself) at ease.

Find a quiet place, somewhere you like the surroundings, i.e. a sunroom or a favourite room in your house.

Make sure it is a time of day when you won't have too many disturbances.

You can perform this exercise sitting or lying down it doesn't matter.

Close your eyes and just say to yourself in a gentle voice relax, relax and then breathe, in and out, in and out saying relax to yourself. You are directing this at your mind and you want to reduce the chatter and noise that your conscious mind generates.

As you are telling your mind to relax, allow your body from the head down to begin to relax, down your forehead, your eye lids, checks, lips, chin, your neck, into your shoulders, down your arms, elbows, into your hands and fingers, down your torso, into your pelvis, hips, buttocks, legs, knees, shins, ankles, feet and toes.

Try and envision a wave of relaxation running down your body, as you breathe in and out, in and out gently. While doing this if you feel any tension in your body due to stress or a physical condition, try just release this bock by focusing on relaxing and releasing within the area where you are experiencing any discomfort, while continuing to gently breathe in and out, in and out and saying relax and release. Imagine the wave of relaxation gently coming through the area in your body where you are experiencing any discomfort or dis-ease, and that area being relaxed and at ease.

Do this exercise for about 5 minutes and you will feel relaxed and at ease. This exercise is a good way of releasing dis-ease within your mind and body.

In later books we will talk about energy and how it runs through your body, and how you can use focus points within your body called Chakras, to enhance energy flow and heal physical conditions.

We will also talk about EFT (Emotional Freedom Techniques), that can help release phobias or habits you want to stop, as well as some QT (Quantum Touch) energy based healing processes.

However it is important to point out here, that anything thought here in the way of tools, techniques or methods, are only in relation to helping you change how your think or release negative thought patterns, as it is thought, negative thought that causes blocks in your body's energy field, and reduces the flow of energy through your body.

To get an idea of what I'm talking about here, put your index finger on your left hand between the thumb and index finger on your right hand and squeeze your index finger on your left hand.

After only a minute or so you will feel the reduced flow of blood, followed by a throbbing. If you kept this up for a long time, the top of your index finger on your left hand would become gangrenous and need to be removed.

This is the same with negative thinking, habitual negative thinking or believes overtime beat up on you, mentally and physically, and over time because there has been a block in the energy flow to certain parts of the body (this is the life giving source energy that supports your physical being) the body begins to develop growths, warts, lumps, cancers, tumours, blood disorders and so on. The body's immune system is weakened too.

However, you now know how to change all of this, don't you?

Pay attention to those emotional feelings you are having, they are the soul, spirit, non-physical part of you communicating with the physical part of you, letting you know the appropriateness of your thoughts, and what they can do for or to you, depending if they are positively or negatively focused.

Perform this exercise throughout the day and make sure you give yourself 5 minutes a few times a day to do this. You can also perform this exercise before going into what you may think might be a stressful situation, or after coming out of one. This could be a work related, relationship or financially related stressful situation, it doesn't matter, performing this exercise helps relax, centre and align you, and you will feel better, guaranteed. Enjoy!

Your primary connection point between the physical you and the non-physical you is through your breath, so breathing slowly and deeply allows a strong connection and allows the sub-conscious mind to be in control as opposed to the conscious mind.

Remember, the sub-conscious mind or the inner you, is one of clarity, calmness and all knowing. The conscious mind is one which can only draw on the experience of your current physical life to date and how it has been programmed or thought how to perceive circumstances and events, and based on that programming reacts in different ways. So breathing, quieting your mind and allowing your body to relax creates a powerful and undiluted connection to the all knowing totality of who you really are.

Become and be
at EASE with
yourself not at
DIS-EASE

Contrast & Variance

L ife is full of contrast, it is full of variance, it is full of difference, and it is through this difference, variance and contrast that life offers you the opportunities for you to decide what you want.

If you see a poor man in the street, you wouldn't have a desire to be poor, you may feel sorry for them, or think how terrible it must be for them, or you may try and give some assistance to them, but in the moment that you see them, there would be a desire in you for more wealth, better prosperity in relation to what you are observing.

If you drive a banger of an old car and you see a nice shiny new racing blue car overtaking you, your desire is not on the old banger you are driving, it's on the nice shiny new car. If you are walking home in the pouring rain from work because you can't afford a car, and an old banger drives past you, your desire won't be on the continuation of having to walk home in the pouring rain, it will be on the old banger that drives past you.

You see it does not matter where you are in life, there will always be something better from your perspective than where you are, and this is the myriad of contrast that we live in.

Now there is another important word that I've being using in this book and in the last few paragraphs, and that is desire.

Desire

here does desire come from? Desire is born out of the contrast of the environment that we live in. <u>It is the observation, or the realization, of something that is different to or considered better than what we already have, or we are already experiencing.</u>

Desire is the summoning forward of the life giving energy that is in each and every one of us, it is the fuel that drives us forward, it is the passion that brings us love, it is the enthusiasm that makes us creative, it is the stuff that gives us inspiration, it is the spirit of life and out of the contrast of life, more desire is born, and it is in the creative force of desire that diversity is perpetuated and the contrast exists, expands and is then experienced and universal evolution continues and grows.

For you are the Universal Power of You, and together we are one co-creative, connected and ever continuing life force, life source energy.

We are the creators, for God exists in all of us, and through each of us, we experience and expand ourselves and the universe, for individually we are unique, and collectively we are one and the same. We are the physical and the non-physical.

Nothing is Perfect

eople will say that nothing is perfect, however, in order for something not to be perfect, it has to be perfect. Perfection lies in the imperfection.

From your current stand point you may say that "this thing that I am experiencing is not perfect, I would much prefer if it was like this instead".

So what we have here is a contrasting scale, think about the car scenario where if you were walking home in the rain and an old banger drove past your, preference would be on driving an old banger as opposed to walking home in the rain. If however, you were driving an old banger and a nice new blue sporty car drove past, your preference would be on the new sporty car.

So the perfection lies in the contrast or in the illusion of imperfection, remember you can't have imperfection without perfection, what you may say is imperfect may be perfect for another, it all depends on where you are and how you are perceiving something in relation to what you desire.

Because there is a contrasting scale in relation to anything, the relationship between you and something on that contrasting scale has the ability to evolve into something that has a more desired preference for you and everyone else too.

Believe It, Manifest It, Live It

Believe in yourself, trust in your inner you, and the feedback and communication you get through your emotions.

Say to yourself "I trust in who I am, and I believe all that I want to be mine ".

Pay attention to how this feels to you. As you become more in touch with your emotions, you will begin to feel the power of that which you really are, you will feel this in the lower part of your abdomen area mostly; however in time you will feel this throughout your body. It will feel like a tingling or fizzing sensation, this will be the Inner You letting you know the inner you is there. Other main areas where you will feel this sensation will be up and down your spine, across your shoulders and in the middle of your forehead.

As you pay attention to how you feel, and make it your intent to feel good most of the time, you become the **oil** that helps all elements of the universe to work with you, in the creation of your life experience and all that you want in it.

It is import for you to realize, that you are the main component in your creation of your life experience, how quickly and easily the things that you want come to you, depends on you, and the better you feel, the more positive and happier that you feel, allows the energy that is at the basis of everything to flow to and through you easily. When you are at ease and going with the flow all things that you want come to you, and this is because you are in a state of allowing, letting it be and letting it all just happen.

So basically the step that you must take is one of alignment, when you line up with your inner you, this means your conscious you and your subconscious you are in sync.

When you achieve this, you will feel an alignment of energy in your body, and this will also be accompanied by the tingling and fizzing sensations.

Mentally, emotionally and physically you will feel a great sense of ease, a great sense of nothing else matters, only that you feel like this – you will feel absolutely amazing.

Your subconscious (Inner You) is always aligned with the super conscious (all that is).

So when you feel this way, you too are now in your physical conscious state of being aligned too with all that is.

When you are in this state of being there is no resistance in you, life flows easily to and through you. Now pay attention to what happens. All the things that you have wanted, and created at the energy level, through your desire, and lined up for you via the

Law of Attraction, and the work of your Inner You now begins to appear out of the blue.

This is because you now from your physical conscious perspective are lined up too. You are now one with what you want, what you've become, and now it is yours to live it.

You may notice that the things that you want in life come when you haven't thought about them for some time. This is because you would have had some resistance to them, maybe because you didn't know where the money was going to come from, and any negative thought would have been blocking what you wanted. However, the very fact that you weren't thinking about what you wanted, also meant that you weren't thinking an opposing thought, or holding any associated negative thought in your vibration, and because of this, what you wanted came.

Relationships

Everything in your life is primarily vibration-ally and relationally-shipped based with yourself.

Everything that you have going on in your life is based on a relationship with something, whether it be a person, an object, an event or circumstance.

To have a good relationship with anything, whether that is a relationship with your lover, your friend, your boss, your money, the material things you have in your life, the main focus of your thought, in relation to any of those people or things must be predominately positive. You need to look for the good in them, in order to get and receive the good from them.

You can't look at the negative and wish for a better relationship, you first have to find the positive. If you can't find the positive, then you need to imagine the positive aspects you want to experience with that particular relationship, and then apply those positive aspects from yourself, towards the very thing that you want to improve your relationship with.

If you want someone to be kinder to you, then you need to be kind in your thoughts, words and actions towards them and all others.

Friendship

Friendship is the base, the foundation for all good relationships. This is the initial building block for all good relationships. Don't be a lover first, be a friend first, then a lover. Don't be a boss first, be a friend first. Don't be a parent first, be a friend first. Don't be a brother or sister first, be a friend first.

When you are a friend first and then build on that, the relationship that you want will be strong and rewarding, because you have put a secure foundation in place.

However, in order to be a good friend to someone or indeed something, you first have to be a good friend to yourself. **You** have to be good to yourself and **you** have to be at ease with yourself and **you** have to put yourself first.

That means first and foremost **your** happiness comes first. In order to give something to another, you have to have it first, so if you don't put yourself first, then you won't really have anything to give to another.

If you want to improve your relationship with money, you have to improve your relationship with you first in relation to money, or any other thing that you want to have. See the following examples of how to improve on your relationships.

Improving my relationship to money, or anything else...

There is lots of money around and I can see the good that it does. I see plenty of people who have money, and all the nice things that it affords them. And isn't it great, that there are so many people who have come into achieving a good relationship with money. I'm gratefully that by seeing money this way, that I too am improving my relationship with money, and with those too who have it, and the nice things that it brings to them.

When you can read the previous paragraph and feel good in the reading of it, feeling at ease in the reading of it, your relationship with money too will improve. It all depends on how you want to look at it (Think about it.)

Now take the subject above on money and replace the subject of money with something that you may want to experience. For example, good health, I see lots of healthy people about, out enjoying themselves, taking walks, going to the gym, running, swimming etc., and so on....

If you want to be slimmer than you are, then you have to improve your relationship with your body and how you think about it.

Example

I like my body, it is such a magnificent thing, it tells me when it's hungry, it tells me when it's thirsty, it tells me when it's cold. It has this amazing ability to process food and turn it into energy to sustain it. It has the ability to take me where ever I want to go. It has the power to think, to evaluate, it has the power to heal itself, it also has the ability to be at its ideal weight, if only I will let it be, if only I will be at ease with it and myself, and not at dis-ease with it and myself.

Improving my relationship with food

When I sit down to have a meal or take a snack, I am going to enjoy the food I put into my mouth, I am going to chew it slowly and appreciate how good it tastes to me, and how it makes me feel. When you adopt this type of mindset, you are at ease with the food and with yourself, and the energy that runs through you, the energy that supports your physical being, flows easily and effectively. If you eat something and beat yourself up over it, you are at dis-ease with the food and yourself, and you slow down the energy, and the processing speed of your metabolism also slows down too.

Also when you are at ease with yourself, there is no desire for you to try and counteract your dis-ease, by trying to comfort yourself with food, or anything else for that matter.

When you are at dis-ease with yourself, and you comfort yourself with food for instance, once you have finished the food, you give yourself a hard time. "Oh, I shouldn't have eaten that, it contains so much calories and I'm trying to lose weight, now I feel bad, where did I put those chocolate biscuits, I need something to cheer me up". Anything seem familiar here, it may not be in relation to food. Your comfort exercise could be to go shopping, and when you do that you say, "Oh, I shouldn't have gone shopping, I didn't need all those clothes, and I've put them on my credit card, and now I'm in more debt and I have less money now as I try to pay off the debt", anything seem familiar here. Your comfort exercise could be drinking, or smoking, but none of these are of any comfort to you, because in the doing of them you feel bad, because you beat up on yourself once you done the action – so if you are being good to yourself, in relation to how you think about yourself, then there will be no need for you to feel like you need to take some sort of action to make yourself feel better, because the action is not the source of the problem, it's the thought that goes before the action.

Am I being my own best friend or my own worst enemy? Well here is the question. Am I being at ease with myself (best friend) or am I being at dis-ease with myself (worst enemy). Your thoughts about yourself (past, present and future ones) are a reflection of who you currently are and are in the becoming of. You are the creator of you.

When you put your relationship with yourself first and decide that no matter what, you are going to be your own best friend, the need to factor in others opinion about you disappears, your opinion on how others think about you disappears, the need to take action to comfort yourself disappears, because when you are happy with you, nothing else will really matter to you, because you feel good about you.

When you are at ease with you, there is no judgement in you, against yourself. However, when you judge yourself, you will judge others in relation to what you are judging in yourself, and others too, will then judge you in return.

Law of Attraction works in every conceivable aspect of your life, and the key to understanding the relationship between you and any other subject or any other thing is your IECGS (Integrated Emotional Communications & Guidance System). How does it feel to you, notice the energy that you feel in your belly, this is how your IECGS communicates with you and gives you the feedback you need to keep yourself on track. Are the feelings you are feeling, feeling good to you?

All the relationships you have are based on how you think about them, and the value that you give them, whether that is a relationship with a person, an object, or even money.

All relationships are created and held in the mind and in this mind you give thought to them, and as you think, you give off a vibration and by law of attraction you are given more similar thoughts on the subject, ones that match the frequency of the vibrational signal you are sending out.

This is why you tend to attract similar and likeminded people into your life. You always hear people saying that they tend to attract the same type of partner (lover, etc.) into their lives. Well that is because of how they are creating those relationships in their mind. Relationships about people, money, the type and satisfaction of their job and so on.

"Why and how come I always attract an abusive lover into my life", sound familiar?

"Why is there always just enough money in my back account, when others have plenty", how about this one, sound familiar?

Remember, your relationships are based on how you think about them, thinking is based on a collection of thoughts, and thoughts are pure energy, the most powerful energy there is.

When you relax with whom you are "Now" you will be all that you have become (vibration-ally). The relationship between you (physically) and you (non-physically) will align up, sync up and your mind, body and soul will be one of a vibrational togetherness and harmony.

The evidence in others of good relationships with themselves

How is it that when I look at others, their lives seem to be so easy? How is it that they have good jobs, nice houses, expensive cars, always seem to have money, the nice girlfriend, the perfect husband, the multiple holidays each year.

How come they go thought life and life seems to be so easy for them. All they want and have seems to come easily and effortlessly to them. It doesn't seem fair, I want all those things too, and I try so hard but I'm not getting the results I want, and if I do get a result I can't seem to sustain it.

If you take a step back and observe how they are acting and behaving, you will notice that when they talk about something that they want, they are talking about it in a positive way, they are noticing the abundance of what life has to offer.

They are talking about how good the thing is that they want. They aren't talking about what they want, and then observing or focusing on the fact that they do not have it yet, or that it is only the privileged few that have it, or those who seem to be born under a lucky star.

They don't bring the relationship of what others have, that they too want, but don't have, into the mix. What they do is to look at what they want and talk about the having of it, and those who have it, and they admire and are pleased for those who have it.

When others who have the stuff that you too want, and you observe how they are acting, and behaving, you will come to the conclusion, that they have what they want through thinking positively about it, and so what they say, and the way they behave, and the actions that they take are defined based on how they think.

The reason why life seems so easy for them is because they have become at ease with themselves, and when you are at ease with yourself, all others and all other things in life become at ease with you, and so life begins to flow easily, and all those things that you want begin to flow easily and effortlessly to you. This is what is meant by going with the flow.

Consider life as one big lake of energy, with lots of different currents in it, each current running in the direction of something that you want. So you pick what you want and jump into that current, and when you are going with the flow you are easily swimming with the current to your destination, when you are not going with the flow you have decided that you will try and swim against the current, and that requires a lot of effort to go in the opposite direction of your destination. I try so hard but get **nowhere**, however when opportunities present themselves and you go with the flow of the current you will be **now-here**. "**no-where**" or "**now-here**" it's always your choice.

This is the difference between positive and negative energy, it's the negative thought that holds you apart from what you want in life. It is the effort of trying so hard to swim against the current.

When you do that life becomes hard, it becomes tiring, you are worn out from it and it **feels** bad to you. When it feels bad to you, this is you (the Inner You) communicating with you, letting you know that how you are thinking, behaving and acting, is not in line with what you want. You need to change your thinking, you need to change your mind.

So what happens when you meet those people in your current for one reason or another that you do not like, are they the rocks in the lake impeding that current that you are on?

That rock may be your boss for instance. However, if you are drifting along in your current and you focus upon the rock, it isn't the rock that will block you it is your focus on the rock that will block you, because the rock is bad and in your way from your perspective.

However, if you were a bird in the sky looking down on the lake, on the current that is bringing you to your desire, you would see that indeed the rock isn't blocking the current, it is however helping to influence that current in the direction of your desired destiny, and so it again depends on how you want to look at it, is the rock impeding you, or is the rock helping you to get to where you want to go, but you just can't see it from your vantage point in the current.

So this is where it takes a little faith and to go with the flow. Pay attention to how you are feeling when you look at the rock, if you are feeling bad then your attention is on the rock and what you perceive it to be or mean to you, and not on the current that is bringing you to what you want.

The Art of Forgiveness

When you are feeling negative (mad, angry, hatred etc.) towards someone or something you are in a negative state of vibration. If you are having ill thoughts towards someone or something you will have ill feelings. This is obvious by now, because those feelings are the feedback to you based on your thinking.

When you have ill will against someone through your attention and your thought of ill will towards someone, you will begin to attract that very ill will you wish for another on to yourself. Remember Law of Attraction works in every conceivable way and you are the creator of your own reality. This is what Karma is, good or bad. You get back what you give out vibration-ally through consistent thought, which leads to behaviour and action. Law of Attraction is the most powerful of all laws in the universe, and Law of Attraction governs all other universal laws, including the Law of Karma.

So forgiving is a very powerful tool to be able to use. Forgiveness is not about you condoning what someone said or did, forgiving is about you letting go of the negative bond, that you have towards someone or something, by releasing the negative thoughts or memories that you have associated with a certain event or occurrence.

Forgiving is you putting you first, so you are able to change the way you feel. Forgiving allows you to feel better about and within yourself, and you now know that how you feel lets you know the appropriateness and correctness of the thoughts that you are thinking in relation to someone or something. The Inner You will never think negatively, for the Inner You has a greater understanding of life than you do from your physical and human conscious awareness.

Forgiving takes practice, remember forgiving is about you feeling better, not anyone else. However, some things are a lot easier to forgive than others are.

So let us address forgiving something that has had a huge negative impact on your life and maybe the lives of others around you too.

First thing here is to put you first, I'm going to start the forgiving process for me.

Let's say you lost a loved one to the intentional or unintentional actions of someone else – This is a big one, so let's see how we get on here.

"But how do I do that, how do I forgive someone that took someone that I loved dearly away from me, why would I want to forgive them".

If this was the case then you would be feeling a lot of mixed ferocious negative emotion, everything from depression, grief, sadness, bewilderment, hatred, madness, resentment and so on.

Your intention for forgiveness is to begin to put yourself a little more at ease, to begin to restore some balance in your life and how you feel.

How do you do that, well there are lots of ways to feel better, her is one.

Start to remember all the good things about the person you lost and just put your attention on that. Remember the happiness and the love you had with that person and just put your attention on that.

Remember, the real you is non-physical conscious energy that can never be destroyed, same goes for the person you lost. While they may not be here physically, they are still very much alive.

When you think of them clear your mind, use one of the tools in this book to do this and help you relax. Remember to breathe and relax. As you do this and by feeling the love you had for this person, you will raise your vibration, when you raise you vibration, you are more closely align to the vibration of Spirit (non-physical) and this will allow you to become connected to that person at an energy level. You may experience very clear pictures of them in your mind, you may even have an audible experience, or you may feel a strong fizzing and tingling sensation around your body. Yes this is them communicating and connecting with you, saying "hello".

You may experience dreams of your loved one, this happens because it is easier for the communication process between the two of you to happen when your conscious mind is relaxed and doesn't have the mix of varying thoughts running around in it.

When you are awake and your mind is fully active, it is like you being in a crowded room with lots of people talking, chattering and making a lot of noise, so it would be very hard for someone on the other side of the room to get your attention, however, when you are asleep (or you calm and quiet your mind), all the people leave the room, it quietens downs, it becomes calm, and then it is easier for the communication process to happen.

As you practice the art of forgiveness you'll find yourself becoming calmer, more balanced, your mind becomes more at ease, you are better allowing the connection with the inner you and through that connection you are connected and more tuned into the energy of your loved one, for the source energy of whom you are they are too.

The Power of Forgetting

Part of the art of forgiveness is the ability to forget. To really benefit from the Art of Forgiveness process, it is now necessary to deactivate the negative thought and emotion associated with what you are forgiving.

Although you may have forgiven someone for what they did or said, in order for you to be completely free of it, it is necessary for you to forget it.

To do this you must learn to release the thought and associated memory.

Each time, for whatever reason you experience something that causes you to associate with the event, or the experience of what occurred, it is now your job to learn to release the memory quickly so it doesn't begin to fester in your conscious mind.

The process for doing this is called release and re-associate.

As you recall the memory you will begin to fell negative emotion, tension and maybe stress.

As this happens recognise what is going on within your thought process, and within how your body feels, and say to yourself, "it's ok", just relax". Take three to five deep breaths (more if you think you need to) repeating to yourself "it's ok", just relax" and allow your mind to clear.

Now take a thought that pleases you (this could be a past experience, something good that you have going on in your life right now, or something that you are looking forward to) and put your attention on that until you begin to feel better and you start feeling positive emotion.

Once you begin to feel better allow yourself to move on to whatever you were going to do.

As you practice this simple process, you will notice that each time the negative memory comes up you will automatically begin to release it, and replace it with a more pleasant thought with little or no effort.

You must remember that you won't be able to remove the impact of the negative memory all at once; this will take patience and practice.

Don't put yourself under pressure to forget, this has to be done bit by bit, once step at a time, there's no rush, you're not on a schedule or trying to adhere to a timetable.

What will happen as you practice this, is that you will begin to replace the negative memory with a positive thought, and that positive thought will become dominate within you.

And because all your thoughts are energy, vibrational energy, with attracting power, you will begin to attract more positive things, people and experiences into your life.

Regardless of the magnitude of what occurred, this process will work, however you must work with the process and be easy with and about it. The aim of this process is for you to be at ease with yourself, in relation to what it is that you are forgiving and forgetting. The memory will always exist, what you need to do is be able to feel better and learn to associate better feeling memories and thoughts. You may find yourself at the starting point in this process of pure hatred and that is ok, what you need to do is move past the hatred and up the emotional ladder to anger and up and up bit by bit.

If your starting point is pure hatred there are two things you do not want to do, one is keeping yourself there by looping back and the second is by staying in the place of pure hatred and slipping down the emotion ladder into depression.

Does It Really Matter

The only reason something really matters to you is because you allow it to. Why do you allow something to matter, well this is because of how you see something to be or the value you hold in relation to something.

In any given situation you have the choice to decide and ask the question, does this really matter to me.

If something has happen and it doesn't feel good to you, remember that based on how you are thinking about it, the inner you is giving you feedback based on the broader perspective of who, you really are.

Many things, large and small, events and circumstances (which ultimately you have attracted) all have a mattering effect on us and our lives. However the degree to which we allow things to affect us (positively or negatively) completely depends on us.

We all have many things going on in our lives, however we tend to allow the little small things be the ones that have a negative impact on us day to day.

If someone hasn't been particularly nice (for whatever reason – maybe they're having a bad day) we tend to let it get to us, but the question is how much does it really matter, how much should we beat ourselves up over it? If someone isn't nice to you at 9:30 am, do you let it go and get on with your day, or do you keep thinking about it, talking about it to your friends or colleagues, are you absolutely livid by 5:30pm, do you then carry this into the next day.

If you've just tidied up the house and your four year old takes out a few toys and starts playing away for a little while and then toddles off to do something else that may take their fancy, and leaves the toys out in the middle of your nice tidy room, do you let it matter to you, does it make you mad?

I've see these types of things happen, where a person really gets heated up over such and similar things, yet I've talked to people who have been in a car crash and the car was wrecked and they'd say, "it doesn't really matter, it could have been a lot worst, someone could have been injured". Yet the same person will get upset over little things like I've mention in the paragraphs above.

You see it all depends on how you've observed or trained yourself to think in certain situations and there are endless amounts of situations that you will experience in your life, so you need to decide on what really matters to you.

When you find yourself in a situation, maybe something similar to the child and the toys, stand back, look at what is really going on, and what is that? Well...

There is your four year old who is everything to you, someone whose happiness and wellbeing really matters to you. What is the child doing? Well he is there playing with his toys, those toys that he wanted and you were only too happy to buy for him and he was thrilled to get them. What is he doing, he's playing, he's having fun, he's enjoying himself. Does that matter, yes it does. Does it really matter that his interest gets turned to something else and off he goes to the next thing and leaves the toys on the floor you just tidied up, no it really doesn't. Never allow something that doesn't really matter, to out weight something that really does, if you do you will feel bad for it.

Ultimately nothing really matters except this - the only thing that matters, is for you and all others to have fun, be happy, enjoy yourself, put your attention on what makes you feel good, nothing else really matters, for when you allow it to, you feel bad, and the choice is always yours.

For the small things that are getting to you, practice the breathing and relaxing exercise, over a little time you will learn to calm yourself and change your mind in relation to how you think.

For the bigger issues that matter (that has a negative feeling or vibrational base) to you, re-read and practice what has been said in the Art of Forgiveness and the Power of Forgetting chapters.

Remember, what you are allowing to matter to you, you are also attracting to you.

Modelling

odelling is the art of taking the successful aspects of someone and introducing those aspects into your own way of thinking, feeling, acting and behaving.

Take a person who has achieved something that you want, but you haven't yet achieved or are having difficulty in achieving what you want.

Observe how they act in relation to what they have achieved. From that point you can begin to relate back how they act to how they must think about what they achieved.

If you know the person who has achieved what you want, simply ask them how they would have thought about the very thing that they achieved.

Did they have a plan, did they seek help, how did they feel towards what they wanted to achieved, did they struggle, were they relaxed in their approached towards it, you get the idea.

If you don't know the person, it could be someone famous on the other side of the world, what you need to do is start to act as if you were them, this takes a little practice and a playful attitude towards this approach.

As you begin to play this out, you will begin to feel like them, as you play this out some more you will begin to think like them.

This is the reverse of what we've been talking about up till now. Up till now we've said you think, feel and act, in this process we reverse it.

To try this out take the person you have in mind and begin to pretend to be them. Do this at home first, for about two to three weeks, as you do this, you will begin to notice that outside of your home you begin to speak like the person, relate to their ideas, you will begin to feel like that person, you will begin to feel a shift in energy, as if you are summoning their energy forward to come through you.

This is true as all energy is connected, and one with everything, so as you begin to act, feel and think like them you summon that energy to you, as it is available to you and anyone else who desires it.

If you want for instance to be stronger in work or meeting situations, pick someone who is positively strong, influential and who is listened to by people, adapt the act, feel and think process and see how you begin to become stronger in this situation too.

You can start making a list of areas you want to improve and things you want to achieve, put names of people you think have the success you want in these areas against your list of areas, adapt the process and away you go.

You will also notice as you model people around you that you will begin to attract more of their attention into your life, and also other people who think and are like minded, will begin to just gravitate into your life.

Be sure you want to have more of these types of people in your life. You need to be clear to yourself and the universe what you want. Do you want to attract a certain aspect of a person, or the person as a whole?

So how do you make the distinction between the aspect of a person and the person as a whole?

If you only want to attract a certain aspect, then only put your attention on the aspect, and don't associate the aspect with the person as a whole.

If however you would like to have more of that person on a whole in your, life then put your attention on the aspect and associate the aspect with the particular person too, as you play out the act, feel and think process.

You will have great fun with this as you begin to notice the difference in you and the way life is responding to you.

Remember, keep this light, keep it fun, by doing it this way the energy that you summon forward will come more easily to you.

You can apply the modelling process to anything, improving relationships, getting the relationships you want, the health you want, the finances you want, better understanding, improving your spirituality, the material gains you desire, the list can go on and on and on, it's up to you.

Remember get into the _Spirit_ of the person, or the aspect of the person you want to model.

Alternatively you can look at what is going well in areas of your own life and begin to apply how you think and feel and the relationship you have around what is going well, and then from that point start applying (the same thinking and feelings) towards that what you want to improve – Simple.

Enjoy yourself!

Inside or Outside

Am I inside or outside the ball, am I alive or dead, am I asleep or am I awake.

Let's pretend that your body is a ball and your consciousness is air and ask the question is the air inside the ball or outside the ball.

Now when you are born or even at the point of conception (depending on the experience you chose to have) your consciousness enters your body, it is like air being blown into the ball and when your consciousness leaves your body, it is the same as letting the air out of the ball.

When you let the air out of the ball, the air does not cease to exist; it just re-emerges back into the air that exists outside the ball.

Now imagine the ball (your physical body) and the air inside the ball (your consciousness – non-physical you) is connected to a super/mass consciousness (the air outside the ball – all that exists non-physically) through the air valve.

Now imagine that the ball has trillions of air valves (cells) and each valve is a point of connection to the air outside the ball (super/mass consciousness).

When your body physically dies (the ball), your consciousness (the air inside the ball) releases itself out through all the trillions of cells (valves) back into the non-physical or super/mass consciousness of thought energy that exists.

So you can see that you, from a consciousness point of view are always connected to the super/mass consciousness, and your inner you, is always connected to the broader perspective and intelligence of that super/mass consciousness of vibrational thought energy.

So, if from a human consciousness perspective you thought you were on the outside trying to look in, you now realize (and one day science will connect with and prove spirit), that ultimately, you were on the outside looking into the outside and inside looking out from the outside as your existence exists simultaneously from both opposites – this may take you a while to get this one, but when you do get it, you will understand it.

So the inner you is really also the outer you, and the outer you gives feedback to the inner you in the language of feelings, which lets you know from its broader perspective the appropriateness and correctness of your thoughts in relation to your **human** (physical you – the ball) conscious thoughts and the frequency those thoughts have in relation to what you want.

In My Own Personal Experience

It has been my own personal experience that the things in life that I have wanted, have come quickest when I haven't been thinking about them. This experience pre-dates any self help or spiritually based book I ever read.

When I look back, when I would initially want something and these were usually big things (brand new car, new house, TV's, better career, better relationships, holidays & travel) and so on, I knew I wanted these things, however, because my expectation wasn't particularly high in getting them, my mind was never in the how it was going to come about mode.

Let me talk you through the blended example below so I can share my personal experience with you.

My first brand new car & more

Back in November 1998 there was a car called a Subaru Impreza that I really loved, however, at that time to buy a car like that brand new, insure it and tax it, would have taken most of my disposable income, which would have meant giving up a lot of my social life, something I didn't want to do as I enjoyed my social life too much.

At the time I had worked out how much gross income I'd needed to achieve the net income to afford the car, insure it, tax it and run it, while still maintaining my social life. I didn't hold much hope or expectation in buying the car any time soon; however I loved the car, loved reading reviews on it and watching car programmes that would be featuring it.

At the time I was interested in gaining a promotion to move my career along and to also have more money to afford the car. I'd chased the same promotion three times, and even with recommendations from my team lead to the department manager I was getting nowhere.

I decided to give up trying for the promotion and to look for another similar position with a different company for a better salary.

Not long afterwards I was offered a position with a different company and for a better salary, so I handed in my notice. My department manager asked me why I was leaving and what sort of salary I was being offered.

On the last week of my notice period my department manager called me into his office and put a proposal to me.

He said he would match the salary the other company was offering (which I told a little white lie about) and give me the opportunity to travel and he'd look into a promotion to team lead in three months time.

I took him up on his offer and stayed and sure enough in three months I got my promotion to team lead.

Just after my promotion, a friend of mine within the company, who had moved to a newly opened department, offering training services to people who wanted to learn or improve on their computer application skills, asked me if I'd be interested in providing training two evenings a week with him. This was a great opportunity to earn some extra money towards a deposit on my car.

Just after taking on this extra new role, a newly created management position came up within the department I was team leading in, it never entered my mind to apply for it as I'd only been promoted to a team lead in the last two months, and there were at least fifteen other team leads with years of experience ahead of me.

I was preparing to give a training class one evening and the training manager who I'd worked with some years previously, asked me if I was going for the newly created management position in the department that I worked in during the day. I said no, I didn't see the point. She said that the position would be perfect for me and I should go for it, and so at the last minute I submitted my application.

It was company policy that all internal applicants who applied for a position must be given the courtesy and the opportunity of being interviewed.

Out of a panel of ten, I was sixth on the list to be interviewed. Just before the interview I was told the interview had to be moved, this happened another three times and now I was going to be the last one interviewed. I was beginning to think that the position had already been decided upon and I was only going to be going through the motions.

The day of the interview came along and I was going to be interviewed by the department manager and his boss who I knew well, as he was not only my first manager but also my hiring manager when I joined the company a few years previously. As it turned out on the day of the interview, another manager who I didn't really know was replacing my first hiring manager for the interview and I didn't really like the replacement manager at the time, because from my perspective he always seemed a bit full and sure of himself (turns out I had him all wrong and years later he's now one of my best friends).

Anyway, I decided just to go along to the interview, relax, give it a go and enjoy the experience. I didn't really have any expectations of getting the position, so I suppose the process of going through the interview didn't hold a whole lot of value to me, in other words I didn't care one way or the other, and because of that my mind was clear and my state of being was relaxed.

Well, the interview went incredibly well. I answered all the questions easily and confidently. The creative side of me came out and I was able to offer ideas on how to do things better, my experience from other companies I'd worked in just poured out of me, I felt alive, excited and inspired as I talked and talked and talked.

It also came about during the interview that the manager I didn't like too much, knew quite a few people that we both knew from working in previous companies, who were to put it mildly, characters in their own right. This meant we ended up swapping stories about some of them and having a good laugh during the interview.

About a week later I got a call to come and see the department manager. I knew I was going to find out the outcome of the interview and I didn't hold much expectation of getting the position due to the strength and experience of the other candidates.

Again, I was the last one to be called. When I went in my manager said, "I'm talking to you last as I thought it only fair to let the unsuccessful candidates know first that they didn't get the position". I thought to myself is he really telling me what I think he is telling me. "Congratulations Alan, you got the position." I was almost stunned out of existence, but there was more to come. When he told me the salary, it was the exact amount I'd worked out that I needed to buy, insure, tax and run the car I wanted, while still having the money to have my social life.

I got my promotion in May 1999 and took delivery of my new Subaru Impreza on June 14th 1999.

I'm still amazed at how life orchestrated the chain of events that was required, that not only got me the new car without having to sacrifice my social life, but also gave me the opportunity to travel while also improving my career and my income considerably.

This is just one of many of these types of experiences I've had in life. All of these experiences happened without my knowledge of Law of Attraction, Vibrational Frequencies, the Physical and Non-

Physical Universe, the Inner You, Emotions and Feelings or a lot of the topics I've talked about in this book.

What I had discovered that worked for me, was when I saw something I wanted and didn't think too much about it or more accurately, how it was going to come about, what I wanted came quite quickly, with little or no effort and for no real apparent reason, it just seemed to happen.

If you look back at the example of the experience I talk about above, you will see, how not getting the promotion initially to team lead, led me to look elsewhere. When that happened my manager took some notice and decided to take steps to hold on to me.

The training department opened which gave me the opportunity to not only gain experience in training but also the ability to earn more money.

The training manager was very influential in helping me to decide to go for the newly created management position.

The company policy to always give the opportunity of an interview to an internal candidate ensured I got an interview.

My interview being moved four times and putting me to the end of the list, ensured that the interview happened with the replacement manager who I synced up with in terms of being able to relate to other people he knew and had worked with before. This helped me to establish something that we had in common during the interview. As it turned out two things were key to getting that promotion that led to better career opportunities, travel and of course the car I loved.

The first, because the interview had been moved four times and I wasn't fixated or expecting to get the promotion, I was in a relaxed state of mind and in that state of being there was no stress, no pressure, no anxiety, no worry – No Resistance. In my state of no resistance I excelled, I was creative, I held nothing back. My mind wasn't worrying about the what if's or what the interviewing managers were thinking, I was in a true state of inspirational allowing, I was in a true state of being me.

The second was that I'd blown the socks off of the replacement interviewing manager (he told me that a few days later), not just from a job interview perspective, but with the connection we'd made, based on our shared relationships with past colleagues from different companies and the experience those relationships afforded me. It was the replacement interviewing manager that helped convince my department manager to give me the position, even though it would probably raise some difficult questions due to the wealth of experience being held by other candidates.

So, if you too look back at things you have achieved easily and breakdown the events and your current thinking or lack of it at the time, you will realize that life is setup to respond to your desires easily. You will see that the process of life and achieving your desires is actually an easy one. Life is supposed to be easy; it's just lack-full or negative human thinking that complicates and slows down the process.

By the way, if I had of actually taken the job with the new company, instead of all of the above positive stuff happening and picking up my new car in June of 1999, I'd have been out of a job in June 1999 as the company I was to go to closed its office.

I hope the above story helps you get the subtle and un-intrusive way that Law of Attraction and life works for you and with you.

There was a point in 2002 where I had a need to try and understand and figure out how and why life worked the way it did and so my journey into spirituality started. I began to attract the knowledge I was looking for, and to my amazement in 2005 I found that there was actually something behind and orchestrating the events and circumstances I had experienced. It was called or explained as Law of Attraction.

When I discovered this thing called Law of Attraction, I was so excited, because I was able to start relating my experiences to it. I did the very thing and continued for quite some time practicing the very thing I shouldn't have been doing. I started to try and make things happen, I started to expect things to happen, and while expectation is a good thing once you understand fully the Law of Attraction, usually when you expect something to happen you put a timeframe on it, and if it doesn't happen within that timeframe you begin to doubt it will happen. So just relax and allow what you want to happen, it will, you just need to let life sort it all out for you, and when something feels right, you need to go in the direction of it.

Don't worry about things too much, even if you think you've made a mistake or taken a wrong turn, be comforted by the knowledge, that all roads lead to where you want to go.

In Summary Book 1

Putting it altogether

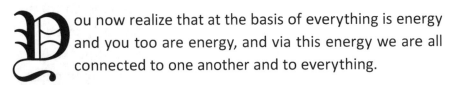ou now realize that at the basis of everything is energy and you too are energy, and via this energy we are all connected to one another and to everything.

You also understand that all energy is vibrational, vibrating at different frequencies.

You now get that energy attracts energy that has matching vibrational frequencies.

You know the type of energy you are attracting by paying attention to how you feel, as the non-physical part of who you are, gives you feedback based on your non-physical broader perspective, understanding and view point.

While there are many different types of feelings and emotions, you now know that all these feelings and emotions fall into two categories, one feels good and the other feels bad, the degree of the feeling depends on the habitual thinking and maturity of the associated thought.

You now also know that those feelings you have, as long as you are paying attention to them, helps you guide your thoughts.

The thoughts that you are thinking are at the base of everything that you have going on in your life, it's up to you to take the time to deliberately choose the thoughts that you want to think in relation to anything that you desire.

Once you've decided on what you desire and how you want to think about it, you have to focus positively on the desire, however that doesn't mean thinking about the desire 24/7. It just means anytime you think about the thing you desire, you are positive in your thinking about it. Be playful in your imagining of the thing you desire, keep it light, don't concern yourself with how or when it will come about, Law of Attraction is figuring all that out. The best thing you can do when you are thinking about something you want, is to get into that feeling place of it, and hold yourself there for as long as it pleases you.

For instance, if you buy a book online, you don't start trying to figure out how it's going to come, for you understand that the handling, shipping and post systems and process will do all that for you, Law of Attraction is exactly the same.

Have you ever considered why some people have fantastic natural ability? Well that's because natural ability is the lack of resistance to what is being focused upon. What that means is, as you see some very gifted sports person pulling off something that seems spectacular, in that precise moment they are focused on the outcome, they aren't thinking about what may or may not go wrong, they aren't considering all the variables of the mays or the may nots, they have put all their attention on what they want to do in that particular moment.

So the same applies to any desire, don't setup resistant thoughts, and if they do enter into your mind you now know you can easily release them.

Know what you want, let the Law of Attraction work it all out, and allow what you want to happen, by keeping yourself as happy and joyful as you can. No one else can upset you, or have a negative influence in your life, unless you allow them to, and that is entirely up to you.

As you read, get, understand and practice what is in this book, over and over again, the information here will begin go percolate into you consciousness and then become part of your believe system which will mean that the practicing of what is being told to you here will become natural to you.

Life, your life and the experiences you are having revolves around how you think, for you are the centre of your own universe.

Enjoy who you really are, be happy with who you really are, be at ease with yourself, be your own best friend, put how you feel first, Love you first, for it's all primarily about you, for YOU are The Universal Power of You.

To touch on the importance of Soul (The Inner You)

The soul of who you are decided to join you in your physical conscious life experience. From your physical perspective as you go through life, all the experiences that make up your physical life are then added to the numerous life experiences of your soul.

The purpose of your soul is to help guide you towards what you want and to guide you toward making the right decisions and also how to beneficially interact and help others too.

Your soul has a defined life purpose too and one of the measurements of success in terms of what your soul has intended in any incarnation, is how it has influenced you and helped you cope throughout your life.

So the conscious physical you need's to recognize that your soul is on a journey too, and so it is of tremendous benefit for you to work with your soul and recognize the communications from your soul to you.

Decide now today, to tell your soul that you are going to work and cooperate with it and help it achieve what it has intended to achieve as part of this life experience.

Once you do that, there will be a unified collaboration between the physical you and the soul of who you really are, and together you can have a very satisfying and rewarding life.

Cooperation between people is the mechanism that joins us together; it is the mechanism that brings us all in the direction of where we desire to go.

When you cooperate with someone or allow someone to cooperate with you in moving towards a desired outcome, you become the key cooperative component in your own life experience.

When we cooperate with each other on a physical level, the energy that joins us together (non-physically) then flows easily and so do we, collectively and individually.

When you look at another from the perspective of soul, you will only see the divine beauty in that person, because the soul of who you are is looking at itself in another.

If you look negatively at someone from your human conscious perspective you will feel negative emotion. This is because how your soul sees the person and how you see the person is out of alignment.

The physical, conscious and individual you, is a part of the being-ness of God (or whatever you hold God to be) experiencing himself and expanding herself, through the collective individual perspective of the physical, conscious and individual US – You and I.

God is the source of who we all are and everything is, recreating itself at every level of consciousness from the unique perspective of everything.

A little bit more...

Quality of thought is universal in its scope and application. The degree of success that is achieved in relation to any subject, is based on the appropriateness of the scope (of thought), and the correct application and depth (of thought), applied to obtain the desired result (the very thing you want).

Quantum Physics is the Science that from a human conscious perspective is Spirit proving itself.

Science is based on data, it's based on evidence and it's based on proof. If something can't be proved scientifically, all that means is, that science (from the human consciousness perspective) hasn't caught up with the very thing it is trying to prove, but don't worry, it will, it always does. The proof of what is being told in this book will be in the evidence of your life experience. So take a step back and look at what is going on in your life, and the data (all the varying bits of your life and what and how things are happening and going on in it) will be all the proof that you need.

The most important piece of data you can ever possess is how you feel.

At the beginning of the book we broke the physical down into the non-physical, we talked about wave packets which comprise of an infinite set of component waves. These waves contain the existence of all possibilities and probabilities. These waves are made up of vibrational energy vibrating at different frequencies and this vibrational energy is what effects the manifestation of matter. So how are these waves effected and what defines the probability of a possibility happening. This happens through conscious thought – conscious thought is what starts the process of collapsing the wave packet. Once the wave packet is collapsed, this then forms a quantum and so the manifestation process starts to create the physical out of the non-physical. To create something you want or the essence of it, you must intentionally focus your attention on the creation of what you desire. Through observing your contrasting environment and putting your attention on something (wanted or unwanted) you become the Observer, Creator and Participant of your own reality.

You are always asking for something through the vibration of thought, the universe it setup to respond to that vibration – The Bible says "Ask and you shall receive."

Some Nuggets of Wisdom

1. _Relationships_ - When you improve your relationship with yourself and become your own best friend all of your other relationships will improve too. How to improve your relationship with yourself – Take all others out of the equation and just be happy with where and who you are right now

2. _Forgiveness_ - Forgiveness is not about condoning. Forgiveness is about releasing the negative bond that holds you in a negative state of being.

3. _Desire & Contrast_ - Your contrasting, diverse, varying environment produces desire and desire is the fuel of life. Stay connected to the feeling of your desires

4. _Success or Failure_ - If you don't achieve a goal, have you failed? No, ultimately there is no such thing as failure, only degrees of success. Don't set the outcome as the goal; allow the goal to be the experience of the journey on the way to the desired outcome. When you set a goal it is achieved instantly vibration-ally. The degree of success is always embedded in the allowing of the experience, of the journey, on the way to the

outcome. So your true goal isn't in the outcome, it's in the allowing of the physical experience of it.

5. _Consciousness_ - From our human need to break things down and label them, so we can better understand or explain something we have layer-ified and labelled consciousness into differ states, conscious, unconscious, subconscious, mass consciousness, super consciousness & supra consciousness. Ultimately, consciousness explained, is the blending, layering and awareness of the eternal existence of a universal infinite array of energy based, thought based consciousness with contrasting vibrational perspective-ness

6. _The Mirror_ - Your thoughts about yourself (past, present and future ones) are a reflection of who you currently are and are in the becoming of. You are the creator of you.

7. _Perspective_ - When you consider the perspective of another you broaden your own.

8. _My Powerful Mind_ – has the power to be limiting or LIMITLESS – Which do you chose.

9. _Breaking you down_ – Body, Bones, Organs, Cells, Molecules, Atoms, Electrons, Protons, Neutrons, Quanta, Quantum, Wave Packets – Energy

10. _Points of Connection_ - The Human Body has up to an estimated 100 trillion cells; every one of those cells is a connection point to Universal Conscious Energy.

11. *Everything is Energy and Energy is Everything* - Universal Conscious Energy flows to you, thought you and around you. Connect with it and you will connect with all of who you really are – EvERYthiNG

12. *All little bit of Quantum* - Blending the Science with the Spiritual - Quantum Physics suggests that at the subatomic level all points in space are essentially the same, and therefore nothing is actually separate from anything else. This is referred to as non-locality - What these tell us is that, at the heart of our universe, there are no separate parts to anything, and that everything is connected to everything else. So we in our physical bodies are connected to all others via the conscious, intelligent and eternal energy that makes up and supports our universe(s).

13. *Possibilities* - In order for something to exist the opposite of it must simultaneously co-exist too, so all possibilities currently exist within you.

14. *Attraction Process* - Desire IT, Feel IT, Allow IT & Attract IT

15. *Tuning in* - Everything that exists offers a vibrational signal/frequency. To attract something you need to tune into that vibrational signal/Frequency. To tune into that vibrational signal/frequency, you must Feel Good about what you want to attract. Practice feeling your way towards what you want as opposed to trying to think your way towards what you want. When you are in that good feeling place with the absence of thinking, you won't set up any resistance. How do you

get into that good feeling place of what you want - Love it, Welcome it, get into the Spirit of IT.

16. _Life_ - Our continuous emergence into Physical and our merging back to Non Physical are evolving points on OUR eternal creative life experience

17. _Welcoming_ - If there is something you want in life but don't yet have, then start by loving and welcoming the very thing you want into your life.

18. _The Road_ - All roads lead to where you want to go. Follow the road of least resistance. The way you do that, is to keep your mind free of clutter.

19. _Manifestation_ - Manifestation is the allowing of that which is firstly spirit (vibration) into the physical

20. _Stress_- Stress is a state of mind, created by the thoughts you think from the environment that you are observing and allowing to influence you.

21. _Happiness_ - What really matters is you and your happiness, first and foremost allow your happiness to come first, allow it to come from within you, because that's where it really is all of the time. Don't allow something that you want, to matter too much to you, don't let your happiness be dependent on your wants. When you are happy for no apparent reason, your happiness is coming from within, which in turn allows the things you want (from without) to come easily to you through a lack of matter-ness. When you are happy (which is a high vibrational state of being) all of who you are – Mind – Body & Spirit is aligned. Happiness

first and nothing else really matters. Happy, Happy, Happy, Happy, Happy ☺

22. _Let it Go_ - If you have a negative thought, don't resist it, don't wrestle with it, just smile and gently let it go.

23. _Problems Vs Solutions_ - In a universe of endless possibilities where the opposites of all those possibilities simultaneously co-exists, if a problem exists in your life, then the solution must also exist too. If you have a problem then life has a solution to it. In letting go of the problem you will become part of the solution, if you continue to focus on the problem, you remain part of the problem and the problem will remain. You can be the problem or the solution. Now which do you choose?

My name is Alan Di Felice and I hope you enjoy reading this book over and over again. I've had a fantastic time on my continuing journey of figuring out and experiencing life. It's been in the writing of this book that I'm now really beginning to get life, understand life, and that is another important tip, in order to truly understand something you have to get it first (those ah ha moments), "I get it, now I understand".

The best way to have those ah, ah moments, is to think of a question you want the answer to, or a solution to a problem you are experiencing and then calm and quiet your mind. When you do this, there will be an uploading of information from your sub-conscious mind (the inner non-physical you) to your conscious mind (the physical you).

The Universal Power of who you really are is always with you.

Before I go, well at least for this book, earlier I talked about you being the oil in your life, and that oil is what keeps all those interacting and inter-related cogs of the Law of Attraction going in terms of what you want, the best way to keep that oil fresh and slippy, and allow those things you want to come easily, is to give LOVE to the very thing that you want, when you are imagining and being in the spirit of what you want, as if you already have it (physically), boost the whole creation process by offering the highest vibration you can, and that highest vibration is one of LOVE. Feel *LOVE for the very thing you want and welcome it into your life*.

www.theuniversalpowerofyou.com

You are the Universal Power of You and the Creator and Centre of your own Reality, indeed your own Universe.

Reader's Notes